Bible Study Series

Nehemiah
Man of Radical Obedience

Marie Coody
Linda Shaw
Helen Silvey

KANSAS CITY, MISSOURI

Copyright 1999

by Beacon Hill Press of Kansas City

ISBN 083-411-8203

Printed in the United States of America

Cover Design: Marie Tabler

Library of Congress Cataloging-in-Publication Data

Coody, Marie, 1925-
    Nehemiah : man of radical obedience / Marie Coody, Linda Shaw, Helen Silvey.
        p. cm. — (Wisdom of the Word Bible study series ; 2)
    ISBN 0-8341-1820-3 (pbk.)
    1. Bible. O.T. Nehemiah Textbooks.   I. Shaw, Linda, 1951-
    II. Silvey, Helen, 1931-   . III. Title.   IV. Series.
BS1365.5.C66 1999
222'.807—dc21   99-25025
                                                              CIP

10 9 8 7 6 5 4 3 2 1

Contents

About Wisdom of the Word

Introduction to Nehemiah

L E S S O N   1

L E S S O N   2

L E S S O N   3

L E S S O N   4

L E S S O N   5

L E S S O N   6

L E S S O N   7

L E S S O N   8

L E S S O N   9

L E S S O N   1 0

About Wisdom of the Word

Wisdom of the Word (W.O.W.) was founded in 1986 by Jeannie McCullough in Bethany, Oklahoma. It began as a weekly Bible study at Bethany First Church of the Nazarene. In the first year the study grew to over 400 members, and women from other churches and the community began joining. The local enrollment of Wisdom of the Word eventually exceeded 1,000 and has included men, women, and children of all ages and many denominations. Wisdom of the Word has been an instrument in uniting the community of believers as well as reaching the unchurched and the lost. It is now ministering to thousands through videos and cassette tapes and other programs such as Children of the Word, prison ministries, and missions.

About the Name

W.O.W. began as "Women of the Word." Then when men began to join in the study with the women, Jeannie changed the name to Wisdom of the Word, not only to retain the W.O.W. acronym, but also because it reflects the mission:

To have our lives visibly changed by gaining wisdom from God's Word and responding in radical obedience to His voice.

About Jeannie McCullough

Jeannie McCullough is a pastor's wife, mother, and grandmother. Her life and ministry have taken her to Bethany, Oklahoma, where her husband, Mel, is the senior pastor at Bethany First Church of the Nazarene. She understands firsthand how radical obedience to God's Word can change a life.

Southern Nazarene University granted Jeannie an honorary doctorate in 1997. Due to her humor and honesty as well as her unique insights and application of the Scriptures in daily living, she is in great demand as a speaker throughout North America. Jeannie strives to be a "salt tablet" who will make others thirsty for God's Word. As she has committed herself to being a student of the Word, God has given her many opportunities to share what He is teaching her.

About the Authors

This is the second study book presented by Wisdom of the Word. Nehemiah naturally follows the history of Ezra, published by Beacon Hill Press of Kansas City in study-book form earlier this year.

A team of three writers joined together to write lessons for this particular study:

• LINDA SHAW was the solo writer for the book of Ezra. She is the mother of Jonathan, Jenny, and Daniel. Linda is a licensed clinical social worker and began the W.O.W prison ministry at a women's prison in the Oklahoma City area.

• MARIE COODY has been an integral part of the W.O.W. study since its beginning in 1986. She and her husband, Darwyn, have two grown daughters and are enjoying retirement.

• HELEN SILVEY is from a family of writers. She is a widow with four grown children. Helen has been a group leader for W.O.W. for many years and is very active in the life of Bethany First Church of the Nazarene.

Interested in starting a W.O.W. Bible study?

If you are interested in starting a W.O.W. Bible study, attending a study in your area, or ordering additional materials, please contact the W.O.W. outreach office in Bethany, Oklahoma, at 1-405-789-2050.

Introduction to Nehemiah

Passion for God's Word and Work

Nehemiah was a man with a passion for God's Word and work. His job as a cupbearer to the king held prestige, and the income was good. His responsibility was to be present at court to hand the king his wine. The cupbearer always tasted the wine first, because if it were poisoned, he would then die instead of the king. Nehemiah's occupation gave him intimacy with the king and an opportunity to advise at the king's request. It's true that he was living in a foreign land, but he had great power by having the king's ear.

Nehemiah means "comfort" or "compassion of God." He was a man of great energy and self-denial who was able to withstand plots laid against the Jews by others. He was a man of action who encouraged, confronted, motivated, supervised, faced injustice, led, organized, managed, met opposition, and persevered. Nehemiah was a contemporary of Ezra, and we see these two men ministering together at the reading of the Law (Nehemiah 8:1-9). Nehemiah exhibited many leadership qualities, including vision (2:1-3) and foresight (2:5-8). He was also compassionate (5:6-11), was a man of prayer (1:2-11), and displayed organizational skills, common sense, and faith (4:20-23).

Susa (or Shushan), the capital of Persia, is where the Book of Nehemiah opens. This was the city where the king resided, located about 100 miles from the Persian Gulf. Earlier, the Babylonian Empire had held Babylon as the capital. While Babylon was still prestigious, Susa had the greatest significance in the Persian Empire at this time, since it held the richest and most important treasures of the empire. This was the location where all military decisions were made; therefore, the city was greatly protected.

Persia, the most powerful nation on earth, had a far-reaching network of roads that allowed for an efficient postal system and quick conveyance of reports. The empire was prosperous, with an intricate system of tribute and taxes. All religions were tolerated as 23 ethnic groups tried to live together in harmony. Art was borrowed from all the other cultures who influenced society—Greek, Egyptian, and Babylonian.

The Persian Empire struggled to be united. Mountains and desert divided the Iranian plateau, making it geographically separate. Also, two lifestyles were represented in Persia. The nomads, who lived on the plateau, were very different from the settlers in the city. Because of the differences in geography, lifestyles, and 23 cultures, unity was difficult. The capital city of Susa was truly the melting pot of the 400s B.C.

During this time, the king of Persia was Artaxerxes, who reigned from 464 to 424 B.C. in Susa. He was the son of Xerxes who took Esther to be his queen (Esther 2:17). Artaxerxes received a letter from Rehum and Shimshai telling him that the Jews were *rebuilding that rebellious and wicked city* of Jerusalem (Ezra 4:8; 4:12). They were reportedly restoring the walls and repairing the foundations (4:12). Rehum and Shimshai warned Artaxerxes that he would no longer receive his tribute from Jerusalem if it were rebuilt and suggested that a search be made for a decree from his predecessors regarding the city (4:13-15). They

As you begin each day, use this acrostic to help you study:

Wait for the Holy Spirit to teach you as you read His Word.

Obey what God instructs you to do.

Remember to praise God for insights and promises fulfilled.

Discover for yourself the incredible faithfulness of God!

succeeded in having the work stopped by the king's order until a search could be made for a decree.

Nehemiah was in the palace serving the king as his cupbearer when the news of the stoppage came. Nehemiah's kinsman Hanani came to report that upon receiving the king's letter, Rehum and Shimshai and associates *went immediately to the Jews in Jerusalem and compelled them by force to stop* (Ezra 4:23). What Hanani told at court was that these men had torn down the wall and the foundation that were being rebuilt and burned the gates to the city. They had totally ruined the work that had so faithfully and carefully been done. This news broke Nehemiah's heart. All the effort and time given by this struggling band of exiles was wiped out by a single order. He felt their discouragement and disappointment. That day Nehemiah's heart took on the burden of rebuilding Jerusalem. He believed the burden was a call from the Lord to take leadership in the completion of the work.

Some believe the Books of Ezra and Nehemiah were originally combined into one book. It is generally agreed that Ezra wrote the Book of Ezra, but there are three main theories given as to the authorship of the Book of Nehemiah. Some scholars believe that it was written by Nehemiah, since much of it is written in the first person. Others contend that it was written by Nehemiah and edited by Ezra. Finally, some theorize that Nehemiah was written by Ezra from Nehemiah's journal. Although we don't actually know the identity of the author, we can be certain the information came directly from Nehemiah's memoirs.

Thirteen years had elapsed since the Book of Ezra ended and Nehemiah's account begins. The first part of the Book of Nehemiah is autobiographical. Nehemiah gives a personal report of his own activities, which, along with Ezra's writings, supply most of the historical information regarding the Jews from 438 to 430 B.C. The book covers a 14-year period from 444 to 431 B.C. As far as the Jews are concerned, the Old Testament gives no further information regarding their history.

Nehemiah actually brought back a third set of captives whose specific purpose was to rebuild the wall around Jerusalem. The first remnant came 100 years before Nehemiah, and the second remnant came with Ezra. After the report from his kinsman Hanani, Nehemiah requested permission from Artaxerxes to go to Jerusalem. The king appointed Nehemiah to be governor, and he served two terms. These terms were interrupted by a visit in 432 B.C. to report back to Artaxerxes.

When the report came that Nehemiah's people were in distress in Jerusalem, he responded. This small, economically depressed desert town was surrounded by enemies. Rebuilding the wall would not be easy, but Nehemiah loved God's Word and His work more than anything else, including his great job and position in Persia. So he answered God's call and went to Jerusalem to help his own people, God's people. While there, he overcame many difficulties and obstacles in order to see that the work was done.

Nehemiah was obviously a man who had a passion for God's Word and His work and was determined to do his part. His actions could be compared to a modern-day situation in which a person with influence, status, and income suddenly decided to leave his career to rebuild a city in a third-world country. He is a man worthy of study, for Nehemiah set his heart right and his priorities straight at great personal sacrifice.

May each one of us be encouraged and blessed as we study the life of a man who loved God's Word and His work.

Written by Linda Shaw

Nehemiah

LESSON 1

■ A study of Nehemiah 1—2:10

DAY ONE

Survival

Read Nehemiah 1, concentrating on verses 1-4.

1. Give the setting (date, place, and people) with which the Book of Nehemiah begins (verses 1-2).

2. If the books of the Bible were in correct chronological order, the other books related to the Persian empire—Daniel, Esther, and Ezra—would come in that order before Nehemiah. Read the following scriptures and record as much of the setting as you can determine, including who is king, on the time line.

   Daniel 8:1-2
   Esther 1:1-3
   Ezra 1:1

   Daniel   Esther   Ezra   Nehemiah

3. What was the specific news from Jerusalem in Nehemiah 1:3?

4. Why do you suppose it was important for a city to have a wall and gates?

5. Look up the following scriptures and record the teachings concerning the importance of a wall.

   1 Samuel 25:15-16

   Ezra 9:9

   Psalm 122:7

   Proverbs 18:11

   Proverbs 25:28

6. Describe the wall and gates in the new Jerusalem, when it will be the perfect city. See Revelation 21:10-14.

MEMORY CHALLENGE

Isaiah 60:18

No longer will violence be heard in your land, nor ruin or destruction within your borders, but you will call your walls Salvation and your gates Praise.

(NIV)

In the middle of November, by our calendar, Nehemiah heard about the pitiful condition of Jerusalem. Remember that Nehemiah was living in Susa, the capital of the Persian Empire, with many other Jewish people. He was probably born in captivity and had grown up hearing the story of how Mordecai and Esther had saved the Hebrew children from annihilation when she pleaded with her husband, King Xerxes, for a reprieve (Esther 7:3-4). Nehemiah knew of Zerubbabel, who had taken the first exiles back to the homeland of Israel to rebuild Jerusalem. He was probably personally acquainted with Ezra, who led back the second set of exiles 13 years before Hanani brought his report. But then, to his amazement, he discovered the structures of Jerusalem were run down and that the walls and gates were broken down. The people were in *trouble and disgrace* (verse 3). Those in the city of God were not surviving very well.

Ezra, a priest and scribe, was called to rebuild the Temple. But who would rebuild the wall and gates? The wall and gates around any city at this time in history had a rich tradition and important purpose. Babylon had been considered the impregnable "wonder city" of the ancient world. The wall around the city was 300 feet high, 80 feet thick, and went 35 feet below ground. It had 250 guard towers and a moat running alongside it. No one could defeat the city of Babylon, it was believed, because of the great protection this wall afforded. Yet when God so willed, the Persian army cleverly entered the city by the Euphrates River and overran the Babylonians. However, the concept lingered—a city was safe only if it had a great wall of protection around it.

We all build walls in our lives too. Some of them serve a very important purpose, for our lives also need to be protected. The physical walls of our homes give us shelter from the weather, animals, and criminals who would seek to do us harm. The mental walls of our brain provide us with the ability to reason so we don't make poor decisions or forget to take charge of matters important to the care of our loved ones. The emotional walls of our lives allow us to ward off hurtful comments or cope with grief. The spiritual wall of the Holy Spirit gives us discernment so that we are not led astray by false teachings. These walls are put in place by a loving Heavenly Father who does not want us to be vulnerable to everything that comes our way. He wants to give us the tools we need to survive in an evil world.

But we also build walls of mistrust, walls to avoid intimacy, walls of judgment, walls of snobbery, walls of revenge, and walls of fear. We may think these are walls of protection we need for survival. But just as Babylon fell, these kinds of walls will be our downfall.

God doesn't want us to merely survive, He wants us to live! He wants us to build only the appropriate walls and embrace each other. He wants us to trust Him with which walls to build and which walls to march around seven times and break down (Joshua 6:20). He will speak to us to clarify which walls are which. Nehemiah was to break down the wall of living in Susa where he was safe and go to an unsafe land to build a wall of protection for God's people.

When Nehemiah heard the news about Jerusalem, he became burdened. That was the beginning of his call. That was when he began to move out of the "survival" mode and into the "trusting God with my life" mode. No more walls of protection, comfort, or money. By faith, Nehemiah began trusting God to be the Wall around his life. God would be the Wall who would empower Nehemiah to complete the job.

Gordon MacDonald is a modern-day Nehemiah. He built the wall of a good reputation as a well-known Christian speaker, author, and pastor. *Ordering Your Private World,* probably his most famous work, is a book that many would benefit from reading. Yet, in an unguarded series of events, his wall was broken down. He broke his marriage vows and had to come to grips with his own weakness and sin. But as a man with a heart for God and His Word and work, he confessed his sin to his wife, family, and friends, and then submitted his resignation to his congregation. For the next year, he and his wife lived in a simple home called Peace Ledge in New Hampshire. There Gordon MacDonald began to rebuild the walls of his life by confessing, studying God's Word, praying, and trying to find ways to minister to others. In a spirit of humility, he put himself under the accountability of others. By being withdrawn and silent, his hope was to heal and rebuild. Then, when he was ready, God could once again use his life.

Rebuilding his wall was a slow process. But through the power of God, Gordon MacDonald put his life back together, brick by brick. He needed the support of friends and family just as Nehemiah had, but he also needed faith and courage. Today, Gordon MacDonald ministers again, but he has a new understanding of broken walls and rebuilt lives.

This would be a good time to think of a wall you have built that is not pleasing to God. Confess it and let the Holy Spirit instruct you. Also, think of a wall you have built in your life that is pleasing to God, and thank Him.

Sat Down and Wept

Read Nehemiah 1:4-7.

1. What did Nehemiah do when he heard the news of Jerusalem's ruins?

2. What is your initial reaction when you hear bad news?

3. Nehemiah not only gave us a model of prayer in the first chapter but also gave us a model of handling grief. When he received the bad news, he first dealt with his emotions, then took an action step. In the following scriptures, specify how these two steps are used.

   1 Samuel 1:9-11

   1 Samuel 30:3-8

   John 11:17, 35-44

4. What happens to us when we only express our emotions without moving ahead to take the action step of praying to the Father?

5. Consider how prayer is affirmed in 1 Thessalonians 5:17-18 by recording that scripture.

6. Tomorrow we will look more closely at Nehemiah's prayer. For today, lay the groundwork by summarizing how the prayer begins in verses 5-7.

Don't you just love the way the Bible lets us see people as they really were? Nehemiah received terrible, heartbreaking news. God, through His inspired Word, did not hide the very human reaction of this man but chose to tell us that Nehemiah wept. How normal, real, and honest!

Many of us have been raised to hide our emotions, whether they be sadness, anger, or even joy. But Nehemiah gave us a wonderful example of how to display our God-given emotions and then deal with them. He wept and allowed himself to grieve. But then he moved on to deal with the situation, first by praying and fasting and later by acting on what God instructed him to do.

Nehemiah was grieved to know that no one had taken charge of this situation in Jerusalem and accomplished the rebuilding of the wall and gates. *Isn't it true that we cannot build until we are greatly concerned about the ruins?* Being greatly concerned about an issue or situation relates to how much we allow ourselves to be aware of our feelings. Nehemiah heard about the ruins because Hanani, knowing that Nehemiah cared, brought him the report. Nehemiah was not afraid to express his feelings. He sat down and wept. He allowed the Lord to burden him. But Nehemiah knew how to deal with his sorrow. He responded to bad news appropriately by grieving and then going to prayer. In his grief, he sought the Lord's help, knowing only He could correct the situation.

Nehemiah's prayer was probably spoken in the privacy of his own home. Several months probably passed from the time of his original prayer to the time he requested permission to go to Jerusalem. But this situation reminds us that when we pray, God helps us make decisions that are pleasing to Him, and the details will fall into place.

MEMORY CHALLENGE

What will no longer be heard within the land or borders?

Success

Read Nehemiah 1:5-11.

1. Nehemiah starts his prayer with acclamation and then confession. Summarize verses 8-9 of the prayer.

2. Compare Nehemiah 1:7-8 to Deuteronomy 30:1-5.

3. Would you say verses 8-9 contain a promise? If so, what is it?

4. In the conclusion of Nehemiah's prayer (verses 10-11), what did he request for himself as a servant of God?

5. Compare Nehemiah's prayer to Daniel's prayer in Daniel 9:4-19.

6. Do you think Daniel also concluded by requesting success for himself, God's servant?

7. Do you remember a time when you prayed for success? If yes, what was your request and how did God answer?

Nehemiah began his prayer by praising God and giving Him glory. Then he confessed the sin of his people. Humbly he included himself in this confession. Nehemiah did not blame others. Instead, he prayed, *We have acted very wickedly toward you* (verse 7). Nehemiah then recommitted his life and the lives of God's people, the Hebrews, to Him. Finally, he requested success when he approached the king to ask permission to leave.

Nehemiah did not just pray for the ability to cope. He did not pray for success just for himself, but he wanted success for God's work. We often pray for what we want or think we need. We might pray about money or a problem with our children. Often these prayers are self-serving, intended to bring comfort into our lives or at least free us from our discomfort. They may have nothing to do with God's will or God's work. But Nehemiah was praying that he be used as an instrument of God to bring about the restoration of the wall and gates at Jerusalem. He knew it was God's will for these to be restored, and he was offering himself as a humble servant.

When doing work God has laid on your heart, pray for success. You are God's servant, and in fulfilling your call, it's not self-serving to ask for success. This is God's work. He wants our efforts for His kingdom to be blessed many times over. Hold nothing back in prayer. In God's work, pray for success!

MEMORY CHALLENGE

"No longer will _____ be heard in your

_____, nor ruin or _____ within your

_____, but you will _____ your walls

_____ and your gates _____."

Isaiah 60:____

Sadness of the Heart

Read Nehemiah 1:11—2:3.

1. What is the last thing Nehemiah tell us in chapter 1?

2. When Nehemiah gave wine to the king, what did the king ask him?

3. What are some reasons given in scripture that we may have sadness of the heart?

   1 Samuel 1:10-18

   1 Kings 21:1-6

   Mark 10:17-22

   Luke 24:17-21

4. Why did Nehemiah have sadness of the heart?

5. What is the value of sadness of the heart? Look up the following scriptures.

   Ecclesiastes 7:3

   2 Corinthians 7:8-11

It's interesting to note that Nehemiah didn't introduce himself until the end of the first chapter. This tells us he was humble and did not have a self-serving attitude. But he finally acknowledged the fact that he was cupbearer to the king. As cupbearer, Nehemiah's job was to taste the wine before giving it to the king, which gave him unique access to Artaxerxes. He had an opportunity to be in the king's presence and to advise him. If the king liked his cupbearer, they probably became good friends. Thus, cupbearers could easily have an influence on the king.

It's very likely that the king had several cupbearers. From the dates given in Nehemiah 1:1 and again in Nehemiah 2:1, we gather that it was three to four months after the report from Hanani that the king questioned Nehemiah about his sadness. It's possible that Nehemiah did not serve as cupbearer during that time or that he had simply used those months to pray in preparation for the opportune moment to tell the king of his burden. Maybe it was a day he could just not help showing his feelings because the burden had become too great. Whatever the reason, Nehemiah's sadness of heart was evident.

Nehemiah is such a godly example of a man of action. He took his sadness and used it for good. He took his position as cupbearer to the king and used it for good. He combined these two in his plan to correct a situation that was displeasing to God. It was a risky plan in many ways, but Nehemiah was determined. Through prayer he came up with a plan, and he proceeded to pursue a course of action. He was also bold enough to ask God that the plan be successful.

Norma was a modern-day Nehemiah who received a plan through prayer and proceeded. With great sadness of heart, she felt she did not love her children as she should. She brought that to the Lord. He said, "Norma, act as if you love them. Live your life in love even if the feelings aren't there." So she did that. For seven long years she just obeyed God's plan, even though in her heart there was sadness. Then one morning she woke up and realized she genuinely did love her children. God had filled her sadness with joy, for she had obeyed and He had given her the desire of her heart.

Wherever you are today with your sadness of heart, don't leave it there. Bring it to the Lord and ask Him for a plan. Let Him give you one, and then have the courage to follow it. Pray for success, and He will accomplish these things according to His will for you.

MEMORY CHALLENGE

What will our walls and gates be called?

Send Me

Read Nehemiah 2:2-6.

1. What does Nehemiah admit in verse 2?

2. Does God have a plan for our fear? Record the following scriptures.

    Psalm 27:1

    Isaiah 41:13

    2 Timothy 1:7

3. The Lord has assured us that we don't need to fear because He will take care of us. Nehemiah believed this and chose to act with _____. Record the following scriptures.

    Deuteronomy 31:6

    2 Chronicles 32:7

    Psalm 31:24

4. Before Nehemiah answered the king, what did he do (verse 4)?

5. What happened in Nehemiah 1 to lay the groundwork for this prayer?

6. Nehemiah had a vision of what he needed to do. What did he ask the king?

7. (Personal) How have you handled a vision that God has given you? If you are comfortable doing so, share this with your group.

When the king saw Nehemiah's sadness of heart, he immediately asked him about it. This brought fear to the heart of Nehemiah, for one of the requirements of being in the king's presence was joyfulness. A person could not enter the palace if he were in mourning. Because lack of joy might indicate discontent with the king himself, the king could fire or execute anyone who displeased him. Therefore, Nehemiah was taking a risk by showing sadness in the king's presence.

In his memoirs, Nehemiah admitted his fear, but he did not let that fear stop him. When we allow fear to control us, we are not allowing God to work. We can be assured that when God calls us to a task, He gives us the strength and courage to complete it. Nehemiah responded with courage but was also wise enough to breathe a quick prayer. In modern-day terms, we could say that Nehemiah "paged" God. This is the first of eight "pages" to God in the Book of Nehemiah. In that quick "page," Nehemiah probably reminded God of the long conversations they had been having regarding the ruins of Jerusalem. They had devised a plan, and now that the plan was set in motion, Nehemiah sent a "page" to say, "Here we go, God! Help!"

Nehemiah had a prayer bank account from which to draw. He had just spent three to four months praying and fasting about the situation in Jerusalem. He had been given a vision and was willing to carry it out. Then when the moment came, it was already "covered" by the prayer account. A quick "page" to God was all that was needed.

Recently a woman had an accident that disoriented her for some moments. She did not know what had happened—her mind could not take it in. But she was a dedicated Christian who started every day with prayer and Bible reading. In that moment of confusion, she did not know what was wrong, but she knew something wasn't right. Her first words were "Jesus, help me." Why? She had a prayer account and could be protected from an overdraft with a quick "page."

As the plan unfolds, we find that the king reacted favorably toward Nehemiah and granted his request. But we must not overlook the fact that Nehemiah was actually willing to go to Jerusalem. When God gives us a vision, He calls us to accomplish it. Many times others will be involved with us—helping us, praying for us, and supporting us. But when He calls us, He expects us to take courage and respond in obedience and faith, not to send someone else in our place. This is called Christian leadership. Nehemiah was given a vision to rebuild the wall and gates of Jerusalem, and he accepted it by saying, "Send me." He was not sent forever. He was sent until the work was completed. Commentators believe he lived about 13 years in Jerusalem and then returned to Persia. Some visions may last a lifetime, or, like Nehemiah's, they may just be a significant portion of one's journey. But Philippians 1:6 reminds us that *he who began a good work in you will carry it on to completion until the day of Christ Jesus.*

MEMORY CHALLENGE

What does the memory challenge mean to you personally?

Safe Conduct

Read Nehemiah 2:7-10.

1. What did Nehemiah request from the king in verses 7-8?

2. What was Ezra's approach to safe conduct? Review Ezra 8:21-23 if necessary.

3. Do you think it was all right for Nehemiah to accept an army escort from the king, whereas Ezra depended solely on God? Why or why not?

4. Do you believe that each of our journeys may be different and that God might require one follower to obey one way and in a similar situation allow another follower to obey differently? (Assume we are not addressing any of God's basic laws.)

5. God resources us and gives us safe conduct also. How does He do this? Record the following scriptures.

   Micah 3:8

   John 16:13

   Ephesians 1:17-19

6. The Holy Spirit is to be our guide through life to give us safe conduct. Try to think of an example in the last year of your life in which He has done this for you.

7. Two major characters in the Book of Nehemiah are introduced in verse 10. Who are they?

Once again, we catch a glimpse of how God worked out His plan for Nehemiah. Previously, when King Artaxerxes had looked into the history of Jerusalem, he wanted the work of rebuilding to stop. Now, on Nehemiah's word alone, he allowed the work to resume and even gave Nehemiah letters of safe conduct as well as letters for resources when he arrived.

For this dangerous journey, which could last three to four months, Nehemiah asked for letters of safe conduct and even accepted an escort of the king's army. Yet when Ezra made the trip, he felt he should depend on God alone for his safety. This is an example of how the Holy Spirit works in our lives. While God's laws are the same for everyone, sometimes we find ourselves in situations we might call "gray areas." In these instances, we must depend on God's Spirit within us to tell us what to do. In Luke 18:18-24, the rich young ruler asked Jesus what he must do to inherit eternal life. Jesus told him that he must sell everything he had and give it to the poor. Possibly not all of us would have received the same answer, however. The rich young ruler apparently had a problem with money; he put his wealth before God. But we may have a weakness in the area of pride or judgmentalism, so the Holy Spirit would lead us in a different way.

We need to accept those differences in each other and "leave the driving" to God. Perhaps Ezra had difficulty depending on God for protection, and the Lord was strengthening his faith muscles in that area. Maybe Nehemiah did not have the same problem. So we see that situations can be similar, yet God will lead us differently. However God leads us, we can always be assured of safe conduct.

The date of Artaxerxes' decree to rebuild the wall and gates of Jerusalem is the beginning of Daniel's 70 weeks (Daniel 9:24). This bit of prophecy is quite important to the Christian world. Gabriel appeared to Daniel and told him there would be 70 sevens (or 70 weeks) for his people, the Israelites, to atone for their wickedness and disobedience to God. Then the Anointed One would appear (verse 25). The time span from the date of Artaxerxes' decree to the time when Christ presented himself as the Messiah in Jerusalem on Psalm Sunday was 69 weeks (a week represented seven years). The 70th week symbolizes the seven years of Tribulation and is yet to be fulfilled (verses 26-27).

In Nehemiah 2:10, the two villains of the Book of Nehemiah appear. Sanballat was the governor of Samaria, and Tobiah was one of his henchmen. They were quite worried about the rebuilding of Jerusalem for several reasons. First, this was the third group to return, which meant the numbers of Jews kept increasing. These men had animosity toward the Jews because Zerubbabel had refused their help. Also, they knew if anyone could rebuild the city, it would be Nehemiah. He had the leadership ability to pull it off, and furthermore, he was backed by the king. All these reasons added up to the threat of power and position to Sanballat and Tobiah. Their fear and jealousy caused them to be enemies of Nehemiah for the entire 13 years of his governorship.

There are always those who oppose God, but the Holy Spirit helps us discern who our enemies are. Some will oppose us. They will doubt whether or not we have listened to God, or maybe they do not listen and oppose Him for their own selfish reasons. Some hope we will fail. We should expect this and persevere. 1 John 3:13 tells us, *Do not be surprised, my brothers, if the world hates you.* But believe this: *the one who is in you is greater than the one who is in the world* (1 John 4:4).

Written by Linda Shaw

MEMORY CHALLENGE

Write the memory verse for this week below.

Nehemiah

LESSON 2

■ A study of Nehemiah 2:11—3

DAY ONE

Ride to Research

Read Nehemiah 2:11-15.

1. What does Nehemiah tell us of his journey to Jerusalem?

2. How long was Nehemiah in Jerusalem before he set out to research the wall?

3. Had Nehemiah told anyone of his plans for the wall?

4. Why do you suppose Nehemiah was the only one on horseback on the ride to research?

5. Imagine that you are a part of the group that accompanied Nehemiah on this ride. Write a paragraph about what you think Nehemiah was trying to accomplish.

6. Write out Luke 1:37. Could this verse be a theme for Nehemiah as he thought about rebuilding the wall?

Listen, my children, and you shall hear
Of the midnight ride of Paul Revere,
On the eighteenth of April, in Seventy-five;
Hardly a man is now alive
Who remembers that famous day and year.
— Henry Wadsworth Longfellow
"Paul Revere's Ride"

A famous midnight ride by Paul Revere took place in our American history. A small nation of upstarts believed that powerful England should not tax their colonists without having some representation in Parliament, their governing body. A chain of events that angered the colonists led them to take a stand. They demanded to be treated fairly. The purpose of that late-night ride was to warn the young nation's people that their stand had been noticed by the English Crown and that troops were being sent to make the colonists comply. Thus the famous words "The British are coming! The British are coming!"

The purpose of Nehemiah's ride was to research a wall meant for protection around a struggling nation that had lost its ability to defend its people. At this point, those in Jerusalem were so despondent and lacking confidence that if Nehemiah would have said, "I've come from Susa to rebuild the wall, and I want everybody to help," the crowd would have responded, "Impossible." Instead, Nehemiah knew he must have

---

MEMORY CHALLENGE

Isaiah 58:11a

*The LORD will guide you always;
he will satisfy your needs
in a sun-scorched land and
will strengthen your frame.*

(NIV)

a plan to present to the people if he hoped to get their support. Therefore, his ride to research was done in secret. He wanted to tell no one what he was doing until he was ready to set the plan in motion. Then he hoped to move so quickly that his enemies would not have time to oppose him.

The author of the Book of Nehemiah chose not to burden us with irrelevant information concerning Nehemiah's trip from Susa to Jerusalem. He just arrived. After resting three days, he took a midnight ride that began at the southwest corner of the city wall at the valley gate and moved eastward up the Kidron Valley. Nehemiah did not go all the way around the city; he just surveyed the critical area. Historical texts have shown this to be the area that was most damaged. There was even a spot where the wall was so broken and crumbled that his mount could not step through it, so Nehemiah had to walk.

To review, remember that Nebuchadnezzar was the one who captured Jerusalem and destroyed it. His troops broke down the walls, burned the gates made of wood, and burned the Temple and palaces (2 Chronicles 36:15-21). But we must think of how this was done, for it leads us to an important point. If you were to destroy a wall of stone by hand, how would you do it? Most of us would try to push it over or kick it, or, if we were on horseback, possibly jab at it with a lance or club. This is what Nebuchadnezzar's army did. What Nehemiah discovered was that the wall was in worse shape than he thought, especially the King's Pool, but all the materials he needed for rebuilding were there. The stones were not gone; they simply were not in place. The resources were available. God and Nehemiah just needed the workers.

The classic American story *The Wizard of Oz* has a similar ending. Dorothy wanted to return to Kansas where she lived with Auntie Em, but she couldn't find the way. She tramped through forests and fields of flowers and challenged the Wicked Witch of the West at her own castle. But in the end Dorothy was told that all along she had possessed the power to return home by simply clicking her ruby slippers and chanting, "There's no place like home." Dorothy had all the resources she needed to achieve her goal. She just didn't recognize it.

Often, when our lives are broken down, all the resources we need for rebuilding are there. The Bible teaches us that *nothing is impossible with God* (Luke 1:37). The plan, the materials, and the workers are all available to us if we research the broken-down area with God. He can give us His plan for rebuilding if we are bold like Nehemiah and confident that God is the Source.

DAY TWO

Readiness to Rebuild

Read Nehemiah 2:16-18.

1. Summarize what Nehemiah said to those in Jerusalem.

2. What was the reply of the people?

3. The people's reply indicated readiness. Look up the following parables and write what you learn about readiness.

   Matthew 25:1-13

   Luke 12:35-37

   Luke 14:17-23

4. Record Ephesians 6:14-15.

5. Write out the following verses from Psalms in the translation of the Bible you use. Then read how they are worded in *The Message*.

   Psalm 53:2

God sticks his head out of heaven. He looks around. He's looking for someone not stupid—one man, even, God-expectant, just one God-ready woman (TM).

Psalm 57:7

I'm ready, God, so ready, ready from head to toe, ready to sing, ready to raise a tune (TM).

Rebuilding often begins with one person's vision. Then others may join in enthusiastically and work hard to help fulfill the vision. We have already been shown that Nehemiah was the man with the vision, but in today's scripture we see his wisdom in administering a plan. First, he appealed to the pride of the people. In the ancient world, broken walls were a symbol of disgrace. These people had disobeyed God; therefore, He had allowed the Babylonians to overrun them. During that time in history, those who did not keep their walls in repair were held in contempt. Proverbs 25:28 states, *Like a city whose walls are broken down is a man who lacks self-control.* This was a serious issue. Second, Nehemiah demonstrated wisdom in administration by giving God the credit for controlling the events up to this point. He wanted the people to know that the gracious hand of God was upon them.

But the point of focus today is the response of the people. They were *ready.* Because God had prepared their hearts, these people immediately responded, *Let us start rebuilding* (verse 18). Probably they were ashamed of the condition of their own town. But for some reason, they were not able to correct it. It was almost as if they were watching and preparing for the moment when God would bring a leader. They showed *readiness.*

A young social worker went to the home of a foster family where, the week before, she had placed a fifth grade boy. When the child saw her, he ran at top speed and grabbed her around the waist for a big hug. He had been watchful all week for someone he knew. He was ready to see a familiar face.

God is still in the business of making our hearts ready. He plants the seed, and often someone else is sent to water it. With a great deal of "Sonshine" we come to the place of being ready to burst into bloom. Our job is to receive the seed, water, and "Sonshine" so our hearts will be ready.

MEMORY CHALLENGE

How often will the Lord guide you?

DAY THREE

Ridiculed

Read Nehemiah 2:19-20.

1. Who ridiculed the Jerusalem Jews when hearing of rebuilding of the wall?

2. David knew how it felt to be ridiculed. Summarize what he wrote in Psalm 44:13.

3. What was Nehemiah's response to the ridicule?

4. David often had a similar response. Summarize the following verses.

   Psalm 7:1-2

   Psalm 35:1-10

   Psalm 59:1-5

5. (Personal) Have you ever been in a situation in which you feel you were ridiculed for being a child of God? How did you handle the situation? Were you pleased with the way you handled the situation, or do you wish you would have done it differently?

Is there one of us alive that at some time in our life hasn't been ridiculed? Once a little boy was being teased on the playground at school. He came home in tears and asked his mom to "go beat those kids up." But she tenderly explained that he was going to have to learn to handle his own problems. She suggested that he try to be tough on the outside like the candy coating on an M&M. But he replied that the mean children had already broken the tough candy coating and that the chocolate on the inside was melted.

Nehemiah, however, gave us a model of how to handle ridicule. He didn't get sidetracked by arguing. That would have wasted energy. Instead he stayed focused on the issue of rebuilding the wall.

While Nehemiah's answer may appear vengeful, as we look closer we see he was really putting the problem in God's hands. He was also being true to his Jewish training by following the Abrahamic covenant, in which God said He would curse whoever curses Israel and He would bless whoever blesses Israel (Genesis 12:3).

Again we see Nehemiah's wise administrative ability. He didn't tell Sanballat, Tobiah, and Geshem that he had the king's permission to rebuild the wall. He was going to let them go to the king and find this out themselves. That could be embarrassing to them, but most of all, it would waste their time. Nehemiah's strategy was to have the wall rebuilt by the time these enemies could do anything about it.

When we begin to rebuild, there may be ridicule from the enemy. Satan loves to make us think that we are too weak or unorganized to accomplish a task God has given us. He loves to put doubt in our minds, not only about our own abilities, but also concerning what God has said to us. Nehemiah was aware of this and would not fall for that trick of Satan. He knew he would be ridiculed. The late Ray C. Stedman, pastor and author, said, "Whenever anybody says, 'I will arise and build,' Satan always replies, 'Then I will arise and oppose.' "

When God has asked you to rebuild, don't lose your self-confidence. There will be those who ridicule. But remember your Source is not your own abilities, but God himself. He has a way to bring success to every plan He has asked of you. *The one who is in you is greater than the one who is in the world* (1 John 4:4).

MEMORY CHALLENGE

Where will the Lord satisfy your needs?

DAY FOUR

Restoration

Read Nehemiah 3:1-2.

1. Who were the first people listed to start the work of restoring the wall?

2. With which gate was the work begun?

3. The symbolism of sheep is prevalent in the Bible. Look up the following scriptures and record how sheep are represented.

   Leviticus 4:32

   Psalm 74:1

   Matthew 9:36

4. Who is the Good Shepherd? Record the following verses.

   Psalm 23:1

   Ezekiel 34:11-12

   John 10:11

5. Who is the Lamb of God? Summarize the following verses.

   Isaiah 53:7

   John 1:36

6. (Personal) What does it mean to you personally that Jesus is the Good Shepherd *and* the Lamb of God?

The *Guideposts Family Concordance* tells us that sheep are animals that are easily influenced or led. We sometimes call them "dumb" animals because they just follow along with no thought as to who the leader is.

Have you ever noticed how many young teens want to look like all their friends? For them, the worst thing they can do is to be different. A few years ago when Reebok tennis shoes were in style, all the teenagers had them. Next, the popular shoe became Air Jordan. Now it's important to wear the Nike brand. A few years from now, all these names may just be a memory, for they will probably have been replaced. This developmental stage in our society, which we call the "teenage years," is marked by one teenager following another. In this way we could compare teenagers with sheep.

We must be careful not to be "dumb" sheep. Wise sheep follow the Good Shepherd. He is *the Lamb of God, who takes away the sin of the world!* (John 1:29). In the Old Testament the term "sheep" was used to describe people as part of a flock who followed God. A sheep was also an animal used for sacrifice for one's sins. It was called a "sin offering." When Christ died on the Cross for our sins, He became the ultimate sacrifice. He was the Lamb of God. As we accept His sacrifice, He also becomes our Good Shepherd, whom we follow.

The first gate to be repaired in the wall was the sheep gate. In the northeast corner of the city, it was the gate that sheep were brought through as they were taken to the Temple to be used as sacrifices. This is where the first people to work on the gate were mentioned. By getting started first, these priests set a wonderful example for others. The sheep gate was also the gate through which Jesus usually entered Jerusalem. This was appropriate, for as the Lamb of God, He was a sacrifice, just as the sheep were.

Our spiritual lives begin with the "sheep gate" in the sense that we are not connected to God until we accept His Son as the ultimate sacrifice for our sins. Our life with God begins at the Cross. *We all, like sheep, have gone astray* (Isaiah 53:6) is another way of saying, *All have sinned and fall short of the glory of God* (Romans 3:23). Today as you study, if you have not entered through the "sheep gate" into a life with the Lamb of God, pause now and ask Jesus to forgive your sins through His sacrifice on the Cross, and allow Him to become your Good Shepherd.

MEMORY CHALLENGE

When needed, what will the Lord strengthen for us?

DAY FIVE

Represents

Read Nehemiah 3:3-32.

1. There are 10 gates in the wall around the city of Jerusalem. List the names of these 10 in the order they are mentioned. The following references will help (verses 1, 3, 6, 13, 14, 15, 26, 28, 29, and 31).

2. On the diagram of the wall on page 8, the sheep gate is written in for you. Moving counter clockwise, write in the names of the other nine gates in the same order as in question 1.

3. Using common sense, match up the name of the gate represented by the description. You may also use the diagram for some hints.

East Gate	Garbage of city was taken from here and dumped
Fish Gate	Led down into Tyropoean Valley
Water Gate	Soldiers rode horses to palace
Old (or Jeshanan) Gate	Merchants from Jordan River, Mediterranean Sea, and Sea of Galilee brought wares here
Refuse (or Dung) Gate	Jugs carried back and forth from Gihon Spring
Fountain Gate	Faced rising sun; access to Temple area
Valley Gate	Registered to enter city here; presented visa
Inspection Gate	Led to En Rogul; spring located where Kidron and Hinnom valleys meet
Horse Gate	Name meant "old"; led toward Ephraim

4. Look up the following scriptures and write the name of the gate represented by these words.

Psalm 23:4

Psalm 139:1

Matthew 4:19

John 4:14

2 Corinthians 7:1

2 Timothy 2:3

5. Record John 10:7 and 9.

6. (Personal) What does Jesus as the Gate represent to you personally?

Jerusalem was a large city where many roads converged. That was the reason many gates were needed. When commerce was good, the gates were hubs of activity. The city council met there, and shopkeepers displayed their wares. When the gates were busy, it was a sign that the city was prosperous.

But nowhere in God's Word do we get such a detailed description of Jerusalem as we do in Nehemiah 3. Bit by bit, we are told the condition of each gate and who repaired it. If we look closely, we notice details. For example, there is no mention of the Water Gate being repaired. That probably means that nothing was wrong with it. But all gates are mentioned and represented by their functions.

Our lives represent a story to everyone around us. When the name of Saddam Hussein is mentioned, we think of a tyrant. Madonna represents a sex symbol. Mother Teresa was a model of goodness and godliness. What do our lives represent?

Doug, a young pastor, felt led to coach a Little League team in a town where there was great competition to be able to play, for there were more players than teams. From the beginning, the Holy Spirit told Doug his coaching was not about winning but about picking children of single-parent families who needed a man to take an interest in them. So that is how he picked his team and set out to represent Christ and love to those children.

The other coaches laughed at his selection of players. They knew that most first-year teams didn't do well, but they kindly advised him to persevere. Doug wasn't worried, because he wasn't concerned about winning but about representing Christ. He worked hard with the players to teach them how to throw, bat, be good sports, and work together as a team. All the time, Doug was loving them.

The kids grew to love Doug and blossomed under his leadership. His team actually won first place in the league, probably because the players were inspired by the coach's love. But even if they hadn't won, this story would still be worth telling, because it's about what Doug's life represented.

People notice. We all represent something. What does your life represent?

MEMORY CHALLENGE

Fill in the blank:

"The Lᴏʀᴅ will _____ you _____; he will _____ your _____ in a sun-scorched land and will _____ your _____."

Isaiah 58:11

Repairs

Reread Nehemiah 3.

1. Do you have any observations about how the repairs were made? Use your own ideas and then also look at verses 10, 23, 28, 29, 30 for a clue about a particular pattern.

2. Making repairs was common in the Old Testament. Summarize the following scriptures.

   1 Kings 18:30

   1 Chronicles 11:8

   Isaiah 61:4

3. How does the Holy Spirit enter into repairs? Record the following verses.

   John 14:26

   John 16:7-8

   Romans 8:26

The people brought about the repairs. Ray C. Stedman preached a series of sermons from the Book of Nehemiah. He made some observations about how the repair work was done. First, he noted that all the people were involved. The only possible exception to this was the nobles of Tekoa. They were from an area on the fringes of civilization about 10 miles south of Jerusalem. There are several theories as to why they were not involved in the work. Maybe they were in sympathy with Sanballat or afraid of him. Maybe they felt that, as nobles, they were too good to work. But they were the only ones who did not help with the repairs.

Stedman goes on to point out that all the people worked together. They also were assigned to work near their own homes. In my neighborhood, there is an island in the street that is full of flowers and plants. It belongs to the neighborhood in general. I've noticed, however, that those who work hardest on it are those who live the nearest. They do most of the planting, weeding, and watering. It is near their home, and they can see the island out their front windows, so they are the most motivated. The same concept of motivation worked well in the rebuilding of the wall. Nehemiah realized that the workers would tend to do a better job and be more enthusiastic if they could see the benefits for themselves and their families.

Finally, Stedman emphasized that everyone completed his or her tasks. In addition, they worked steadily so that the job was completed quickly. Nehemiah was wise in what he asked of the people and how he made the assignments.

Repairs are important to a community. There can be problems in churches or schools or neighborhoods that need to be worked out. But genuine repairs begin within each one of us. *What causes fights and quarrels among you? Don't they come from your desires that battle within you? You want something but don't get it* (James 4:1-2). None of us ever arrive here on earth as perfect. We all must look to the Holy Spirit to make repairs in our lives so we can be the representatives of Christ that we desire to be. Making repairs is hard work. It means letting the Holy Spirit teach us and then allowing Him to remind us whenever we might go back to our old sins. Some repairs are done quickly, but others go more slowly. Having a team to encourage us and hold us accountable will help. Allowing others to be involved in the repairs, working with us, will bring the task to completion. Can we claim Philippians 1:6 too often? *Being confident of this, that he who began a good work in you will carry it on to completion until the day of Christ Jesus.*

When making repairs, timing is everything. Nehemiah knew that the time was right for him to go to Jerusalem and rebuild. He knew his timing for examining the wall should be at night so the plan could be kept secret. When the time was right, he revealed the plan.

It was put into effect immediately so the wall could be rebuilt in 52 days (Nehemiah 6:15).

What if Nehemiah had delayed? It's quite possible that the enemy would have had time to organize. Maybe another nation would have overrun Jerusalem, and the stones would have been carried off to build a palace or temple somewhere else. Perhaps a plague would have overtaken the people, and there would be no one left to rebuild the wall. Indeed, when making repairs, timing is of utmost importance.

When we miss our timing, we lose a window of opportunity that sometimes cannot be regained. If Nehemiah had not answered God's call, the next leader would have had a much bigger problem. Using the examples just mentioned, he would have to haul in stone, find laborers, and while doing so, fight off the enemies. Just as repairs on our homes become bigger jobs when we don't take care of them in a timely manner, repairs in our personal and spiritual lives are affected in the same way. If the Lord has called you to make a repair, don't delay. Timing is everything.

Written by Linda Shaw

MEMORY CHALLENGE

Write Isaiah 58:11a from memory.

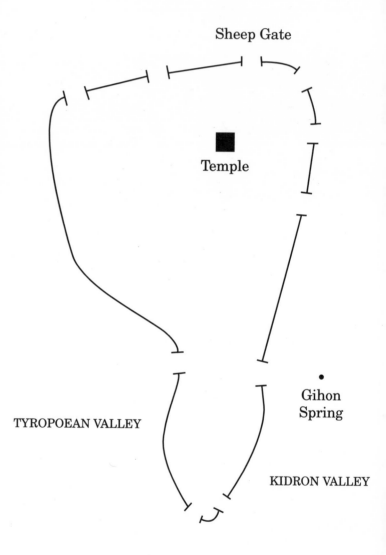

THE GATES AND WALLS OF JERUSALEM

(Nehemiah 3)

Sheep Gate

Temple

TYROPOEAN VALLEY

Gihon Spring

KIDRON VALLEY

HINNOM VALLEY

• En Rogel

Nehemiah

LESSON 3

■ **A study of Nehemiah 4**

DAY ONE

Feeble Jews

Read Nehemiah 4:1-3.

1. What term in verse 2 did Sanballat use to describe the Jews?

2. What did Sanballat ask about the Jews in the presence of his associates?

3. How did Tobiah ridicule the Jews?

4. (Personal) Think back to a time in your life when you were ridiculed. Explain how your self-esteem was affected by the situation.

5. How does God see us? Look up the following scriptures and summarize them to help with your answer.

   Genesis 1:26-27

Matthew 10:29-31

2 Corinthians 3:18

Colossians 3:12

6. How do you think most of us formulate our self-esteem? From where (or whom) do you think God would want us to formulate it?

MEMORY CHALLENGE

Isaiah 58:11*b*

You will be like a well-watered garden, like a spring whose waters never fail.

(NIV)

Sanballat, the governor of Samaria, probably hoped that someday he would also be the governor of Judah (which would include Jerusalem). However, when Nehemiah presented himself as the leader of the people, Sanballat's hopes were dashed. He became angry and brought his whole army to ridicule the Jews. This was simply an act of intimidation because he knew that he could not actually attack Nehemiah, who had Artaxerxes' permission to rebuild the wall. But he thought it was possible to force the Jews to abandon the rebuilding project by ridiculing them.

Sanballat's troops tried to get the people of Jerusalem to believe that their manpower and resources were woefully inadequate for rebuilding the wall. Tobiah discouraged the people further by telling them their wall was so flimsy that it would break down if even a fox were to climb on it. His point actually held an element of truth, because the wall was probably made of limestone. Since limestone is fairly soft, it could easily break or crumble.

The Jews and Samaritans had not been on good terms for about 300 years prior to this incident. When Israel's Northern Kingdom was overrun, most of the people were carried into captivity. The few who were left intermarried with other captives brought to the land by Sargon of Assyria. These people repopulated the country and were called Samaritans.

The Jews wanted nothing to do with the Samaritans, because their race was impure. According to God's law, intermarriage was a sin. We can see that the relationship between the Jews and the Samaritans had further deteriorated by the time of Christ. Undoubtedly, some were surprised when Jesus reached out to the woman at the well, since He was a Jew and she was a Samaritan (John 4:9). Also, in Luke 10:25-37, Jesus tells the parable of the Good Samaritan. It was probably difficult for anyone to imagine a Samaritan being described as "good."

As the chapter progresses, we see that only Nehemiah's strong and wise leadership kept the people from quitting. Being called "feeble Jews" hurt them deeply. They already felt somewhat powerless in this small, rundown city, and being mocked, called names, and intimidated was almost more than they could bear. Many of the Jews had a low self-concept, and the ridicule seemed to hit at the core of what they already believed to be true about themselves.

The people had disobeyed God and their land had been overrun. Restoring the wall was slow and painful work, and it was not progressing very well. They had lost their magnificent Temple and had to settle for a cheap replacement. Many of their fellow Jews didn't even want to return home.

With this background in mind, it's easy to see how even small incidents could have plunged the people into self-doubt and low self-esteem. They were probably already wondering the same things Sanballat questioned them about. We can be certain the name-calling hurt their pride. Tobiah's accusation about the condition of the wall was probably already on their minds. They felt pretty feeble. It only took a few well-directed comments to make them believers.

We aren't so different, are we? At times when we're vulnerable, a few choice questions or comments can adversely affect us. Why not just give up? But God does not expect us to be so influenced by our neighbors. He wants us to receive our self-image from Him.

In our culture, self-esteem for women could come from beauty, being a good mother, or having a good husband, a nice house, or a good job. For men, self-esteem might come from being athletic, having money or status, or having a good job, a pretty wife, or kids who make them proud. But God wants our esteem to come from Him. We are made in His image. That in itself makes us worthy. Then He allows us to call Him Father, and we are to be called His children. We are joint heirs with Jesus. We have no need to be overly concerned about outward appearances. We have esteem in Him.

Do you have a problem with how you feel about yourself? Sometimes we tend to compare ourselves with others, but we need to remember that we are all unique. We each have our own set of gifts and talents to be used by God. When someone raises self-doubt in you, do you feel more unworthy than ever? Look up. Tell yourself that God is your Father, and you are made in His image. No one can ever take that from you. You are a child of the King who has access to the greatest power available. Believe not what people say about you, but believe that you are made like God.

Full Force

Read Nehemiah 4:4-6.

1. Summarize Nehemiah's prayer.

2. Summarize the following verses from Psalms and compare them to Nehemiah's prayer.

   Psalm 35:1-2

   Psalm 59:1-2

   Psalm 69:27-28

   Psalm 79:4-6

3. (Thought question) It seems that both David and Nehemiah, in similar situations, prayed for the destruction of their enemies. How would you explain this? If possible, back up your viewpoint with scriptures.

4. One possible explanation is the Abrahamic covenant, mentioned last week. Summarize this from memory or by looking up Genesis 12:3.

5. Another possible explanation is that Nehemiah and David put vengeance in the hands of the Lord. They did not make it personal. See how this is scriptural by looking up the following verses.

   Deuteronomy 32:35

   Psalm 94:1

Romans 12:19

6. (Thought question) Yet another possibility is that Nehemiah and David felt these people were not attacking them but were attacking God and His honor. That could not be tolerated. Try to find a scripture that would support this idea.

7. According to Nehemiah 4:6, how did the people work?

8. What is the New Testament pattern of dealing with our enemies? Summarize the following scriptures.

   Matthew 5:11-12

   Matthew 5:43-45

   Ephesians 4:32

This is the second time in the Book of Nehemiah that Nehemiah "paged" God. It was a quick prayer in a crisis situation. He could have traded insults, but instead, Nehemiah prayed for righteous judgment. Nehemiah didn't get sidetracked by arguing, because he knew he was doing God's will. He did not get personal but followed the godly pattern in Old Testament times of dealing with his enemies by looking to God for vengeance.

The people succeeded in this seemingly impossible task of rebuilding the wall in 52 days because Nehemiah prayed and because they trusted their leader. But they also succeeded because of what we are told in verse 6—they worked with all their hearts. They worked full force. They gave it everything and would not be deterred.

Working "full force" means we have a passion for what we are doing. We do it because we believe God has put it in our hearts. We don't just go through the motions or plod along, gritting our teeth, to accomplish the task. We work full force because we have an intense desire to get the job done. By working full force, we are working with our whole hearts.

Rudy was a young man who loved football and had always wanted to play for Notre Dame. Everyone told him the idea was ridiculous because his family could not afford it, he was too little, and Notre Dame hadn't recruited him. But Rudy had a dream, and he was willing to work full force for it.

Rudy devised a plan that began with his entering Holy Cross Junior College in order to improve his grades enough to get into Notre Dame. Once at Notre Dame, he worked on the grounds crew for the football field, just so he could get the feel of the field he would someday play on. Finally the day came when the walk-ons (players who were not recruited to play football) got their chance to try out. There were more skilled players than Rudy, but the coaches were impressed because no matter how hard he was hit, he got back up and tried just as hard on the next play.

In the beginning, the first-string players made fun of Rudy; later they resented him for working so hard and making them look bad. But slowly they saw a quality in him they could only wish they had. Rudy worked full force. He had won their respect.

By Rudy's senior year, he had only managed to be a part of the practice team and had never "suited up" for a game. Only the best 60 players are allowed to do that. Rudy's dream was to be on the sidelines in uniform with his teammates just one time. That was what he had worked for with full force.

One of Rudy's teammates went to the coach to ask for this special favor. Then the school newspaper wrote a story about him, telling how he had worked so hard practicing with the team to make the starters better players. It seemed that everyone wanted him to suit up. Because Rudy had worked full force, he was noticed and he was allowed to participate. Toward the end of the game on Rudy's big day, the crowd began to chant, "Rudy, Rudy." The coach put him in the game for the last two plays.

On the last play of the game, Rudy, who was playing defense, broke through the line and tackled the quarterback. Time ran out, and his teammates stormed the field, put Rudy on their shoulders, and carried him off the field. At the time a movie was made of Rudy's story, no other player had been carried off the field by Notre Dame players since 1975.

What an example of working with one's whole heart! And what a legacy Rudy left to his teammates, family, town, and university by doing so. Nehemiah and the Jews did no less.

MEMORY CHALLENGE

If you let the Lord guide you, what will you be like?

Fatigued

Read Nehemiah 4:7-12.

1. What happened in verses 7-8 when the enemies of the Jews heard they were rebuilding the wall?

2. How did Nehemiah and the Jews respond?

3. Summarize Acts 4:16-20. In this passage, Peter and John were threatened by God's enemies. Be sure to include how they responded.

4. What was the complaint of the people in Nehemiah 4:10?

5. External threat plus overwork equals the title of this day's lesson. What is it?

6. List what happened to God's people in each of the scenarios below when they became fatigued.

   Deuteronomy 25:18

   1 Samuel 30:9-10

   2 Samuel 23:9-10

   Psalm 6:6

7. How can we overcome fatigue? Answer this by summarizing the following scriptures.

   Isaiah 40:29-31

   Isaiah 50:4

   Hebrews 12:2-3

8. What is your personal formula for overcoming fatigue?

When ridicule did not work, the enemies of the Jews threatened to attack in order to scare them into quitting. There were enemies on every side. To the north was Sanballat of the Samaritans. To the south was Geshem of the Arabs. Tobiah of the Ammonites was to the east. To the west was Ashdod of the Philistines. God's people felt overwhelmed.

In Nehemiah 4:10, we read that the people were getting worn out. The physical work was quite hard, and they were going at a heavy pace. Between the external threat of enemies and the internal threat of discouragement, the people became fatigued. Fatigue can be paralyzing, because it attacks both the body and the mind.

But Nehemiah had a beautiful formula for overcoming fatigue. The Jews prayed and watched. Instead of looking at the overwhelming odds, they looked at their overpowering God. Nehemiah reminded them of God's plan, goal, and His great protection. Then they persevered. *Let us not become weary in doing good, for at the proper time we will reap a harvest if we do not give up* (Galatians 6:9).

At one time when I was struggling with external threats and physical overwork that led to fatigue, the Lord led me to Psalm 85:8, which says, *I will listen to what God the LORD will say; he promises peace to his people, his saints—but let them not return to folly.* Certainly, there is no peace when we are fatigued and find ourselves in a difficult situation. But God seemed to say to me, "Linda, you do your part. Listen to Me in what I instruct you to do. If you do this, My part will be to give you peace. But you must continue to do your part by obeying what I have said and not returning to the old way of living, which brought fatigue."

It would have been a mistake for the Jews to have given up because of external threat and internal discouragement, which led to fatigue. God makes a way for us to overcome fatigue and be successful in what He has asked of us if we do our part. When I get overwhelmed and fatigued, one of the ways I fight it is by going back and reviewing my part and being sure I'm doing it. Then my peace returns, and with God's help, I accomplish His plan.

MEMORY CHALLENGE

Recite Isaiah 58:11*b* aloud three times.

DAY FOUR

Fear Not

Read Nehemiah 4:13-15.

1. In today's passage, what were the three basic points of Nehemiah's message to the people?

2. The following scriptures have some similar themes. List them.

   Numbers 14:7-9

   Deuteronomy 1:29

   2 Samuel 10:12

3. The Bible does not specifically say what the enemies did at this point, but what do you assume happened, according to verse 15?

4. The *Guidepost Family Concordance* lists "fear not" 51 times. Record three of these reminders below.

   1 Chronicles 28:20

   Isaiah 41:10

   Zechariah 8:13

5. When we are afraid, what should we remember? Record your answers below.

   Psalm 78:35

   2 Timothy 2:8

6. (Personal) To motivate the people, Nehemiah reminded them of their family responsibilities. Would this be a source of motivation for you as well? How?

Once again we are reminded of Nehemiah's strength, wisdom, and godliness by how he handled the latest crisis. He told the people not to be afraid and pointed out that they should remember who they were serving and representing.

In the history of the United States, we as citizens have often been admonished to "remember" during a time of crisis. In Texas's fight over independence from Mexico, the rallying cry was "Remember the Alamo!" Why? Americans considered what happened at the Alamo to be an outrage, because only a few men were present to defend Texas against a large Mexican army. They all became heroes, but they also all died. Americans were angry over those deaths and were motivated to avenge them. When the Japanese bombed Pearl Harbor unexpectedly in 1941, the rallying cry to get into the war was "Remember Pearl Harbor!"

But Nehemiah was motivated by much more than remembered tragedies. He said, *Remember the Lord, who is great and awesome* (Nehemiah 4:14). There was no reason to fear. They were doing the Lord's work. God, as the Great Provider, was in control.

Nehemiah reminded the people of the responsibility they had for protecting their families. What a great motivation! Most of us would be very willing to complete any task if it were for the protection and benefit of our families. As a result of the renewed determination of the people to succeed, the enemies backed off. When you are in a crisis situation, keep in mind the powerful process used by Nehemiah. Fear not, remember that God is in charge and you are serving Him, and let your family help motivate you to do what is needed.

MEMORY CHALLENGE

Draw or paste a picture here that represents to you this week's memory verse.

DAY FIVE

Fortified

Read Nehemiah 4:16-20.

1. When the people returned to the task of rebuilding the wall, how was the work done?

2. Where did the man stay who sounded the trumpet? Why?

3. Record Nehemiah 4:20.

4. This passage teaches that standing guard for each other in the family of God is necessary if we are to be fortified. What are some modern-day ways we can stand guard for each other?

5. Record the following verses, which promise us that God will fight for us.

Exodus 14:14

Deuteronomy 1:29-30

Joshua 23:10

Precautions were taken to ensure that the Jews would not be caught off guard. The workers were heavily guarded, and each one had a weapon strapped to his side. The guards held the weapons in their hands so as to be ready to defend themselves at a moment's notice.

Nehemiah's plan called for half the men to work while the other half stood guard. Farmers and shepherds in outlying, isolated areas requested that workers be brought back from Jerusalem to protect them from attacks. Instead, Nehemiah wisely chose to bring everyone into the town together, making it fortified.

We may not presently be in physical danger, but we need to stand guard spiritually for each other. That is the way we become fortified as Christian brothers and sisters.

One way to fortify the Body of Christ would be for us as Christians to pray for each other. *Devote yourselves to prayer, being watchful and thankful. And pray for us* (Colossians 4:2-3). "Being watchful" in this passage means "standing guard." Colossians 4:12, referring to Epaphras, says, *He is always wrestling in prayer for you, that you may stand firm in all the will of God, mature and fully assured.* We do wrestle in prayer when we are standing guard for each other.

Another way to become fortified is to speak the truth in love. When we see those we are to stand guard for giving in to temptation, we should lovingly confront them to give them an opportunity to turn back. *If your brother sins against you, go and show him his fault, just between the two of you. If he listens to you, you have won your brother over* (Matthew 18:15).

Perhaps you have a good friend who would like to act as an accountability partner with you. Someone who loves us without being judgmental can be a wonderful asset as we strive to maintain a healthy spiritual life. We are fortified when we submit ourselves to a partner who is committed in love to approach us when he or she observes us giving in to temptation. *Whoever turns a sinner from the error of his way will save him from death and cover over a multitude of sins* (James 5:20).

Encouragement is a wonderful way we can stand guard for each other. A word of encouragement lifts our spirits and helps us to persevere. Positive words inspire us to continue what the Lord has directed us to do. Paul told the Ephesians he was sending Tychicus *for this very purpose . . . that he may encourage you* (Ephesians 6:22).

Finally, we are fortified when we lift up God's Word to each other. *Preach the Word; be prepared in season and out of season; correct, rebuke and encourage—with great patience and careful instruction* (2 Timothy 4:2). Jesus prayed to God, *I gave them the words you gave me and they accepted them* (John 17:8). When we share His Word and accept it, we stand guard for each other.

So *be on your guard; stand firm in the faith; be men of courage; be strong* (1 Corinthians 16:13). Then you will be fortified.

MEMORY CHALLENGE

Find a way today to share the idea in the memory verse with someone.

DAY SIX

First Light

Read Nehemiah 4:21-23.

1. How long did the workers toil each day?

2. How much of our time should we give God each day?

3. Do we have to be clergy or in a service profession or heavily involved with volunteer church work in order to give each day to God? Write your personal philosophy about this.

4. Multiple choice: While God wants us to give Him all of our day, which part does He long for us to reserve just for Him? *(a)* first; *(b)* middle; *(c)* last. Summarize the following scriptures to help with your answer.

   Leviticus 23:9-10

   Exodus 13:1-2

   Acts 20:7

5. (Personal) Is giving God "first light" a part of your routine? If you are faithful in giving Him another time of day, He is pleased. But if you aren't currently spending regular time with Him, would you pray now about giving Him "first light"?

6. What do you believe giving God "first light" would involve? State your own ideas. If you need help, you might refer to your notes of the lesson on Nehemiah 1.

7. What is God's ultimate goal in us when we give Him first light? Record James 1:18 to help with your answer.

When you wake up in the morning, do you sometimes dread the thought of another day? You might be going through a difficult season in your life, and memories of an unpleasant situation come immediately to your mind as soon as you awake. Sometimes an illness or other physical discomfort can make us dread getting out of bed.

But God wants us to wake up thinking "It's 'first light'; it's going to be a great day in the Lord!" When circumstances are rough, this is not easy, but if we'll give Him the first part of our day, He'll help us. Reading the Word and praying at the beginning of the day is an activity we can joyfully anticipate. It's a time for meditation and relaxation, and we can expect to be filled up with enough strength for that day.

In my walk with the Lord, I am committed to giving Him my "first light." No, I can't truthfully say that I always concentrate on Him as well as I should, or that I've never missed a day. But spending time with God in the quietness of the morning is a great way to start the day. I try to focus on Him and what He wants for me and my family. I take time to read His Word, meditate on it, confess, praise, thank Him, and present my requests. Then I'm ready to face my tasks and pleasures, friends and family. On days I fail to do this, I never seem to be able to get focused on Him throughout the day. I'm out of sync. I have found that the key to my day is giving God "first light."

Written by Linda Shaw

MEMORY CHALLENGE

A review:

"The LORD will _____ you _____; he will _____ your _____ in a sun-scorched land and will _____ your frame. You will be like a _____-_____ garden, like a _____ whose waters never _____."

Isaiah 58:11

Notes:

Nehemiah

■ A study of Nehemiah 5

DAY ONE

Angry

Read Nehemiah 5, concentrating on verses 1-11.

1. The Jews were crying out against their brothers. They had three complaints. Explain these below, using the verses given as guidelines.

   Verse 2:

   Verse 3:

   Verses 4-5:

2. To understand what is occurring in this passage, some background in Mosaic Law is necessary. Summarize the basics of the law concerning charging interest on a loan to a fellow Israelite.

   Exodus 22:25

   Deuteronomy 15:7-11

   Deuteronomy 23:19-20

3. Now summarize the basics of the law concerning slavery (or indentured servanthood).

   Exodus 21:2-4

   Leviticus 25:39-43

   Deuteronomy 15:12-15

4. For fun, note when this law was probably first disobeyed by looking up Genesis 37:27. Do you remember how God brought good out of that situation many years later?

5. How would the New Testament teach us to handle the issues of slavery and interest rates among our fellow Christians who are poor? Record Philippians 1:27.

Because of their concentrated effort to rebuild the wall, the Jews had literally dropped everything else for 52 days. They had not been able to work on their homes, harvest their crops, or take care of their

MEMORY CHALLENGE

Isaiah 58:12a

Your people will rebuild the ancient ruins and will raise up the age-old foundations.

(NIV)

financial business. The situation had created some real problems, and the people began to complain.

The poverty of the people was certainly a concern. Nehemiah 5:3 tells us that there was a famine during this time, and food and money were in short supply. The landowners were forced to mortgage their property to buy food and pay the heavy Persian taxes. Some of the rich people were taking advantage of the Jews. They were glad to lend money but were quick to repossess land if only one payment was missed. In order to repay their debts, some Jews were forced to sell their children into slavery.

In Israelite society, lending money in itself was not considered wrong, but charging interest was not acceptable. One Israelite was not to profit from the misfortune of a fellow Jew. They were to pull together during difficulties, not take advantage of one another. So although the interest was not outrageous according to today's standards, it was a violation of the law mentioned in Exodus 22:25.

This all probably took place after the 52 days of building the wall. The Jews would probably not have taken time to bring this up, thereby causing a rift during the rebuilding. Also, we can see that Nehemiah's statement in verse 14 is reflective. Even though it happened after the rebuilding, Nehemiah apparently decided to put it here in his memoirs.

With this background in mind, we can understand why Nehemiah became angry. The anger he displayed could be described as righteous anger. Let's explore this thought.

6. How would you describe righteous anger?

7. Now, using a Bible concordance or study book, find a definition of righteous anger.

8. Summarize the following scriptures to help you recognize when righteous anger is appropriate.

Joshua 7:1

Judges 2:11-13

Psalm 78:18-21

9. Did Jesus ever display righteous anger? Summarize the following scriptures.

Matthew 21:12-13

Matthew 23:33-36 (He is speaking to the Pharisees.)

Mark 3:1-6

Nehemiah was angry over an injustice to people. Some of the people were not obeying God's law. Nehemiah knew they would never be blessed in their homeland if this behavior continued, for disobedience was the very reason they had been overrun by Nebuchadnezzar in the first place. So Nehemiah was right to be angry.

Righteous anger could be defined as "anger toward sin." Sometimes we are very comfortable ignoring sin in our culture. But once again, Nehemiah was a model for us, because he was not willing to overlook it. Not only did he confront it, but he showed some emotion when he did. He had reason to be angry.

We as Christians recognize that Christ is our model, but sometimes we fail to look at all aspects of His personality. Christ became angry where sin was concerned. The scriptures in question 9 remind us of the times He drove the evil money changers out of the Temple, displayed anger at the Pharisees who did not want to see a man healed because it was the Sabbath, and actually once called the Pharisees names! Those seven woes he pronounced on the Pharisees in the 23rd chapter of Matthew were strong. In that situation, Jesus righteously revealed His anger.

Often anger is self-centered. We become angry when we are treated unfairly and sometimes we are resentful because we don't get what we want. But Christ, as Nehemiah before Him, became angry because God's laws were not being obeyed.

Accused

Read Nehemiah 5:7-8.

1. What were the two steps Nehemiah took in verse 7 to correct the problem of usury (the practice of charging excess interest) and slavery within the Jerusalem community?

2. Record the definition of "ponder." You may want to use a dictionary or Bible concordance.

3. The following scriptures encourage us to ponder or think deeply and soberly about circumstances in our lives. Record them.

   Proverbs 4:26

   Proverbs 5:21

   Luke 2:19

4. What were Nehemiah's accusations?

5. Look up Leviticus 25:47-48 and imagine what Nehemiah might have been thinking. How does this relate to our study today?

6. How did the people respond?

7. (Personal) Honestly, how do you most often respond when accused?

8. How did Jesus respond when He was accused? See Mark 14:55-56 and 60-61.

Again we are reminded of the wisdom of Nehemiah. Before he responded to this situation, he pondered it. This was serious business, and he intended to give it careful thought before taking any action. Although the Bible does not mention it specifically, we know that Nehemiah was a man of prayer and can assume he prayed about the situation before he came to a conclusion.

Nehemiah knew that in the long run, denial of sin would hurt the community. He decided to bring this evil into the open; thus he helped his fellow Jews escape from a sinful trap. Nehemiah and others had redeemed some of their enslaved brothers as allowed for in the Leviticus passage. But these usurers had sold them back to non-Israelites. They were taking advantage of their fellowman, and Nehemiah was not going to tolerate this among God's people.

Perhaps the most amazing part of this passage is how the nobles and officials responded: they became quiet! It was apparent that God had gone ahead of Nehemiah, for the people were very mature in their response. They did not become defensive. They knew they were wrong and were able to admit it. They responded much as Jesus did hundreds of years later when He was accused.

In our society, it's easy for us to become defensive when accusations are made against us. We try to explain ourselves and rationalize our actions. Even when we are in the right, as Jesus was, becoming defensive is not the best plan. If we do, many times we end up attacking people instead of the problem.

Some time ago a friend of mine was involved in a committee meeting that became very heated. Two other members of the committee were having difficulty working well together. At the meeting, one began to verbally attack the other, complaining that he was causing problems. To my friend's amazement, the accused man sat there silently. He did not get pulled into the argument by trying to defend himself. He simply sat silently while the other man raged on about him.

That was one of the best examples of godliness my friend had ever seen. Probably the accused man could have made some accusations of his own. It's quite likely that he could have explained some of his actions. Instead, he knew it was pointless to argue, and the godly, righteous action at that point was to keep quiet.

Interestingly, because of his silence, the other committee members immediately began to defend him. They were very uncomfortable with the situation and were not going to tolerate it. Whether they realized it or not, the true colors of the two men came out that day. The one who remained silent when accused had a tremendous spiritual impact on the others.

There is a time to accuse when sin is prevalent. There is a time to remain silent when accused and allow God and fellow Christians to be our defense.

Amends

Read Nehemiah 5:9-12a.

1. How did Nehemiah say the people should walk, and why?

2. How did Nehemiah's philosophy about lending differ from the philosophy of the men he confronted?

3. How did the usurers respond?

4. Besides material goods, what other amends were these men willing to make?

5. Summarize the following scriptures, which tell of making amends.

    Exodus 22:1, 3, 5

    Luke 19:1-9

6. In 2 Samuel 12:13-14 we read of a time when David had to make amends because of his sin. Summarize what happened.

Nehemiah's concern that the people were not walking in the fear of God centered around two issues. The first was the charging of interest when this was not acceptable for Jewish brothers, as we studied yesterday. In today's passage, Nehemiah admits he has also lent money and grain to needy people, but either he charged no interest or it was a very small and fair amount compared to what these men were charging. Because these Jews were already wealthy, they did not need the money. Apparently, greed was the basis for their actions. But when confronted, they agreed to give back alienated property and goods received through usury.

Nehemiah's second concern was the reputation of God's people. When outsiders or non-Jews saw how God's chosen people treated each other in hard times, it was a poor witness. They needed to make amends to save

What will the people do?

their reputation. Nehemiah was aware that, *As it is written: God's name is blasphemed among the Gentiles because of you* (Romans 2:24).

We should never be afraid to make amends when we have been poor witnesses before nonbelievers. Sometimes by humbling ourselves and showing our own human weaknesses, we can make a profound impact on others because they can identify with us.

A Christian accountant had been dealing with a complicated case for a client. The client had actually been hesitant to come to this particular individual because of his distaste for Christians but, in the course of service, had come to greatly admire the accountant.

One day at the end of a session, the client asked an innocent but personal question: "Does your daughter live in Phoenix because of her line of work?" The accountant was caught off guard because she did not want to discuss why her daughter lived in Phoenix. So she just answered, "Yes." Actually, because of a major disagreement between them, the daughter wanted to move far away from her mother. On the way home that night, the accountant felt convicted. To save face, she had lied in a professional relationship, which, above all things, demanded trust.

Now the accountant was in a dilemma. She felt she must confess her sin to the client. Yet how would it look for a Christian to reveal she had lied? Would this cause the client no longer to trust her? She was sorry she had gotten herself into such a situation.

But, of course, the only way to correct the situation was to make amends. So at the next work session, the accountant began with confession. The client responded, "Well, it really doesn't matter." The accountant continued, "It does matter that I was not truthful with you. I want you to know that I was wrong, and I apologize. I will try to never fall into that trap again."

Do you think the client had less respect for the accountant after this incident? Probably not. If the accountant was so careful to be honest in such a small thing, then her work ethic surely could be trusted.

The Jewish people had been a poor witness to their neighbors, but making amends could only improve their reputation among the nonbelievers.

MEMORY CHALLENGE

Who was going to rebuild the ancient ruins and raise up the age-old foundations?

Amen

Read Nehemiah 5:12b-13.

1. What did Nehemiah require of the nobles and officials in order to seal the agreement?

2. What symbolic act did Nehemiah perform, and what did he say?

3. Nehemiah's action was similar to a symbolic action in the New Testament. Look up the following scriptures and record what this action was.

   Matthew 10:14

   Acts 13:51

4. Why was it so important for a man to be shaken out from the believers if he was deliberately doing wrong? Give a few ideas of your own; then look up the following scriptures and summarize them.

   Joshua 7:1, 10-12, 19-26

   Acts 5:1-11

   1 Corinthians 5:1-5

5. Nehemiah shook out the sin, but he was willing to allow the sinners to stay if they would repent, promise to refrain from the sin, and seal it with an oath. If a man did not remain true to his oath,

then Nehemiah's symbolic action of shaking out his robe became a curse. For some historical background, summarize the following scriptures.

Numbers 5:19-22

Numbers 30:1-2

2 Chronicles 15:12-15

6. In Nehemiah 5:13, the whole assembly responded by saying, "_____."

7. What does "amen" mean?

In our culture, when we make an agreement or contract, our signature is required. Nehemiah required the officials and nobles to "sign" their agreement by taking an oath. Then the whole congregation sealed it by saying, "Amen." This oath became binding, and as some of the scriptures above revealed, anyone who broke the agreement could suffer severe consequences.

The term "shaken out and emptied" refers to losing all one has. In Old Testament times, it described the act of complete rejection. Even more serious, it was used as a curse on anyone who did not keep an oath. The seriousness of the oath is revealed by the fact that it was administered by the priest. Then it was affirmed by all the people as they replied, "Amen."

What a wonderful reminder of the importance of keeping our word! Whether you make a promise, sign a contract, or take an oath, *Let your "yes" be yes, and your "no," no, or you will be condemned* (James 5:12). And all the people said, "Amen."

Fill in the blank:

"Your people will _____ the ancient ruins

and will _____ _____ the age-old

_____."

Isaiah 58:12a

Allotment

Read Nehemiah 5:14-16.

1. What had the previous governors received as pay for their services?

2. How much of Nehemiah's allotment did he accept?

3. Why didn't Nehemiah take his full allotment or lord his position over the people?

4. Define "reverence" or "fear of the Lord."

5. Record the following scriptures, which admonish us to reverence the Lord.

   Deuteronomy 6:13

   Psalm 33:8

   Isaiah 17:7

6. (Personal) What are some specific ways you reverence the Lord?

7. (Personal) Do you feel convicted in any way that your life doesn't reflect proper reverence for God? If so, jot down a few thoughts about that, and then pray and ask for God's forgiveness. Make an oath to Him that, with His help, you will start to reverence Him in a way that would be pleasing to Him.

The normal allotment to a governor of Judah was 40 shekels of silver a year plus food to serve himself, his family, and those in his work force. This had put a great burden on many of the Jews who were struggling financially. Nehemiah did not ask for the normal allotment, because he was concerned for the welfare of his people. Instead, he devoted himself to the work of rebuilding the wall and provided for his own table.

If he were with us today, Nehemiah would not fit in with our present leaders. In our society we sometimes see politicians, athletes, entertainers, and big businessmen using their positions to get rich. Nehemiah could have made this choice, but he tells us he did not because of his reverence for God. He was not influenced by the accepted practices of the day but did what was right in God's sight.

Yes, Nehemiah was apparently a wealthy man and perhaps did not need the money. But everyone is due a fair wage for the job he or she performs. And Nehemiah had a difficult job with much resistance, which produced great frustration, stress, and discouragement. He deserved to be paid. Yet, knowing that under the circumstances the money simply was not available, he was not concerned about it. He relied on God, not man, for his allotment.

MEMORY CHALLENGE

How does this week's scripture fit in with the study of Nehemiah?

Abundance

Read Nehemiah 5:17-19.

1. How many Jews and officials ate at Nehemiah's table each day?

2. What kinds of food and drink did Nehemiah supply from his own funds each day?

3. Other governors and kings also enjoyed abundant tables. Record the provisions listed in the following scriptures.

   1 Kings 4:22-23

   1 Kings 18:19

4. Nehemiah had a spirit of abundance toward his fellow Jews. What did he ask of God in return?

5. How does God remember us with abundance? Record the following scriptures.

   Job 36:31

   Psalm 132:15

   Matthew 25:29

   John 10:10

6. Give your personal interpretation of the last scripture, John 10:10.

Nehemiah led by example. He didn't acquire land from the people by lending grain or money and then taking the deed when they could not pay. Instead, out of his own pocket, he provided food for more than 150 table guests, including some Jews immigrating to Judah with no place as yet to live.

His motive was to serve God. But as he writes his memoirs or possibly presents them in the Temple, Nehemiah ends this section by asking God to remember him. He has remembered God's people and been abundantly fair with them. Now he simply asks favor in return.

When we live our lives with a spirit of abundance toward others, I believe God is abundant with us. This does not mean that we won't have trials or suffering, but within our circumstances God will provide for us in abundance. Money may be short, for God certainly does not promise abundant finances for us all. But he does promise abundant life.

An abundant life consists of love, joy, peace, compassion, understanding, patience, contentment, and meaningful relationships, among other things. It represents a life so filled up with God that there is no room for bitterness, dishonesty, or whining. It is a life full of faith that God will provide each day what we need emotionally, physically, materially, spiritually, or mentally. It is life lived to the fullest with freedom in Christ.

Consider the old saying, "What goes around comes around." Is that true with God? If we are loving and caring in our relationships with others, does God make sure that we are loved and cared for? If we are generous with our money, does God see that all our financial needs are met? If we are faithful to pray, does God bring answers to our prayers? Do we reap what we sow?

Do not despair in times of testing. In the Book of Job, we see that God allowed Job to go through a very difficult time of testing, during which he questioned many aspects of his life, including his beliefs about God. But God was there with him all the time. Although Job lost a great deal, God honored his faithfulness and rewarded him abundantly. In the same way, Nehemiah wanted God to remember him for the things he had done. As we ask God to let us reap what we have sown, we can trust Him to be abundantly faithful!

Written by Linda Shaw

MEMORY CHALLENGE

Try to put this week's memory verse into your own words.

Notes:

Nehemiah

LESSON 5

■ A study of Nehemiah 6—7:3

DAY ONE

Wisdom Resources

Read Nehemiah 6:1-4.

1. Why were Nehemiah's enemies so alarmed?

2. What construction remained?

3. What message was sent by Sanballat?

4. What was Nehemiah's reply?

Nehemiah's enemies were desperate. Their efforts to stop construction on the wall were failing. Four times Sanballat and Tobiah sent the same message, asking Nehemiah to meet them on the plain of Ono, and each time they received the same reply from Nehemiah: he was busy and could not go. Nehemiah recognized this as a scheme by his enemies to harm him and achieve their purpose by treachery.

The plain of Ono was located 20 to 25 miles northwest of Jerusalem near Lod. It was the westernmost area settled by the returning Jews and was not within the borders of Judah. Nehemiah knew that a trip to this desolate area would put him at the mercy of his enemies and make him vulnerable to murder or kidnapping. Nehemiah was needed in Jerusalem to complete the building of the wall. He was wise enough to remember his priorities and would not be so easily diverted from his primary mission.

5. *But where can wisdom be found? Where does understanding dwell?* (Job 28:12). What answer do you find in Job 12:13?

6. *How much better to get wisdom than gold, to choose understanding rather than silver!* (Proverbs 16:16). Read Job 28:28; Psalm 111:10; and Proverbs 9:10. What do they tell us concerning wisdom and understanding?

7. Summarize these verses:

   Psalm 32:8

   Proverbs 2:1-2, 5-6

   Proverbs 3:5-6

MEMORY CHALLENGE

Isaiah 58:12*b*

You will be called Repairer of Broken Walls, Restorer of Streets with Dwellings.

(NIV)

Isaiah 30:21

8. List three things we must do to receive God-given wisdom. Use these verses to help you with your answers.

   Psalm 37:30-31

   2 Timothy 3:16-17

   James 1:5

9. David's prayers often included requests for guidance and direction. Read these two passages as paraphrased in *The Living Bible*.

   Lord, lead me as you promised you would; otherwise my enemies will conquer me. Tell me clearly what to do, which way to turn (Psalm 5:8).

   Show me the path where I should go, O Lord; point out the right road for me to walk (Psalm 25:4).

Nehemiah was a man of integrity, discernment, and wisdom; he was not flattered or fooled by the offer his enemies proposed. Wisdom is not mere knowledge or education. According to the *Reader's Digest Encyclopedia Dictionary,* "wisdom is the power of true and right discernment" and "the course of action dictated by such discernment." Discernment refers to keenness of judgment or insight.

Nehemiah was a radically obedient man of prayer and knew God and His Word. Quoting the *Oxford Companion to the Bible:* "It becomes evident that he believed in immediate contact with God through prayer . . . *God determined every step that Nehemiah took after his arrival in Jerusalem* . . . Nehemiah never doubted that God was on his side and would finally grant him victory over his adversaries" (italics added).

10. (Personal) Do you seek God's guidance through prayer and meditation on His Word? Are you radically obedient to His will? If you have ever sensed God's direction and, by following it, were kept from harm, share your experience with your group if you are comfortable doing so.

Wrongful Reports

Read Nehemiah 6:5-9.

1. Sanballat sent a fifth message to Nehemiah in an unsealed letter. Why do you think the letter was not sealed?

2. Sanballat claimed that reports were circulating among the nations concerning Nehemiah's activities in Jerusalem. What were these rumors?

3. Sanballat urged Nehemiah to confer with him because *this report will get back to the king.* What was Nehemiah's reply?

4. When you are doing God's work, you may receive unjust attacks on your character. Read these passages and record the false report as well as the name of the person being slandered.

   Genesis 39:7-10, 14-18

   Luke 23:2, 5

   Acts 21:17-29

5. Proverbs 12:5 tells us, *The advice of the wicked is deceitful.* David also experienced slanderous attacks. Record his warning found in Psalm 5:9.

6. Seven sins that are detestable to the Lord are listed in Proverbs 6:16-20. Name the ones that apply to Nehemiah's enemies.

7. Instead of being discouraged, Nehemiah prayed and trusted God. Write God's promise found in Isaiah 54:17.

8. (Personal) Words spoken against us are the most painful attacks we may have to face. Have you been the victim of false reports? How did you handle the situation? Do you wish you had handled it differently?

We know that Satan does not give up easily. He used many tricks from his arsenal to try to cause Nehemiah to fail. He does the same with us; sometimes he succeeds. But God does not want us to fail. He will make His great power available to us if we just ask and trust Him as Nehemiah did. And Nehemiah did not fail!

Sanballat tried to turn Nehemiah's people against him with false rumors. The fact that the letter was unsealed indicates that Sanballat wanted to make sure its contents were made public to discourage the workers. An open letter was an insult. Letters sent to officials during this period were usually written on a papyrus or leather sheet, rolled up and tied, and carefully sealed, sometimes even put into costly silken bags and sealed again. This procedure guaranteed their authenticity.

Sanballat, backed by his cohort, Geshem, made two accusations: (1) Nehemiah and the Jews were building the wall because they were planning a revolt, and (2) Nehemiah planned to become king and had appointed prophets to proclaim his kingship. Sanballat pretended to be informing Nehemiah out of friendship, to prevent this report from reaching King Artaxerxes. Nehemiah not only denied the rumors but accused Sanballat of making up the entire report. Nehemiah had nothing to fear. He knew he was walking in obedience and was able to trust God with his good name.

A young minister was called to pastor a declining church where the members were accustomed to non-threatening, "feel good" sermons. The former pastor had accommodated the wishes of a few powerful members who did not want to be made uncomfortable. The young pastor, however, felt God's leading to preach strong messages on sin, obedience, and disciplined lives. He began inviting the unchurched—people these members considered unacceptable because of the way they dressed or lived. Negative comments became harsh criticism, then escalated to false reports about the pastor's character. The pastor and his family were deeply hurt, but after praying together, they felt God was instructing them to ignore the attacks and not attempt to defend themselves.

The blatant attempts to force the pastor's resignation or dismissal, and his loving Christian response, finally aroused other members to action on his behalf. They began to affirm his preaching and defend him from the false accusations. A few disgruntled members left the church, but this was the beginning of a revival that swept the congregation, revitalizing the lives of the members and winning new souls to Christ.

Do you affirm the spiritual leaders of your church, those who are a spiritual influence to you and your family? Do you regularly lift them in prayer? This week, consider making a special effort to send notes of appreciation to encourage and affirm them.

The ninth commandment (Exodus 20:16) says, *You shall not give false testimony against your neighbor.* Exodus 23:1 says, *Do not spread false reports. Do not help a wicked man by being a malicious witness.* Leviticus 19:16 says, *Do not go about spreading slander among your people.* God has forbidden gossip, whether true or false, and *a false witness will perish, and whoever listens to him will be destroyed forever* (Proverbs 21:28). Have you ever been guilty of spreading rumors? If you have, take time now to ask God to forgive you. *If we confess our sins, he is faithful and just and will forgive us our sins and purify us from all unrighteousness* (1 John 1:9). If you need to ask someone to forgive you, resolve to do it as soon as possible, unless to do so would cause additional hurt.

MEMORY CHALLENGE

Who will be called Repairer of Broken Walls, Restorer of Streets with Dwellings?

Weakness Defeated

Reread Nehemiah 6:9.

1. What did Nehemiah realize his enemies were trying to do?

2. What have you learned in your study of Nehemiah about his first reaction to any need, decision, or problem? For help, refer to Nehemiah 1:4-11; 2:4; 4:4-5, 9; 5:19; 6:9; 13:14, 22, 29, 31.

3. (Personal) What is your first reaction when faced with a crisis? According to Psalm 105:4, how should we respond?

4. What did Nehemiah ask God to do?

5. David also relied on God for strength. *It is God who arms me with strength and makes my way perfect* (2 Samuel 22:33 and Psalm 18:32). And he gave God praise and thanksgiving for giving him that strength. Record these verses:

    1 Chronicles 29:12-13

    Psalm 68:35

    Psalm 138:3 from *The Living Bible* reads, *When I pray, you answer me, and encourage me by giving me the strength I need.*

6. What phrases in common do you find in these verses: Exodus 15:2; Psalm 118:14; Isaiah 12:2?

7. Summarize these promises of God's gift of strength for your life.

    Psalm 46:1

Isaiah 40:31

Isaiah 41:10

Has the enemy caused you to have "weak hands"? The Hebrew idiom "to cause the hands to drop" means "to demoralize." Nehemiah realized that Judah's enemies were trying to frighten and discourage him and his people. Once again, Nehemiah "paged" God in an emergency, with a brief prayer for strength and encouragement for himself and his people.

When we encounter opposition while doing God's work, Satan can make us discouraged and tempted to quit. We may even pray, "God, get me out of this." But Nehemiah's prayer was *Strengthen my hands.* Nehemiah was connected to God's power through prayer and was determined to let nothing prevent him from carrying out the task God had given him to do. When we pray for strength to carry out God's work in the face of opposition, He will not fail us.

In his book *Turn It to Gold,* James Kennedy tells of touring a printing plant where he "saw a mammoth printing press a story-and-a-half high. Huge rolls of paper were fed into this machine and then cut, printed, turned, folded, stamped, and made into booklets at an astonishing speed. This press exuded tremendous power. It was a wonder to behold. Yet all a person would have to do was reach down and pull the plug, and those great wheels would grind to a halt. The lights would go out, the whirring would stop, and that huge machine would just stand here powerless."

Are you powerless because you are unplugged from the Source of power and strength? If you believe God's promises, ask Him for His strength, and trust in His power. God can work through you in spite of your weaknesses. *My grace is sufficient for you, for my power is made perfect in weakness* (2 Corinthians 12:9).

By admitting our weaknesses and relying on God's strength rather than on ourselves, we can accomplish the goal set before us. He is *able to do immeasurably more than all we ask or imagine, according to his power that is at work within us* (Ephesians 3:20).

MEMORY CHALLENGE

Write the memory verse for this week.

Walking in Obedience

Read Nehemiah 6:10-14.

1. What did Shemaiah advise Nehemiah to do, and why?

2. What was Nehemiah's reply?

3. Why do you think Nehemiah would be committing sin if he followed Shemaiah's advice? Read Numbers 3:10 and 18:7 to help you with your answer.

4. About who did Nehemiah talk to God, and why?

5. We must be alert and on guard lest we follow and obey false prophets. Give three ways to identify a false prophet. Use these scriptures to help you with your answer.

    Deuteronomy 18:21-22

    Acts 17:11

    1 Thessalonians 5:17

6. Nehemiah could not be lured into disobeying God. He knew God's Law, and he knew that God had given him the task of rebuilding the wall. He was also a man of obedience. Can God trust you to be radically obedient? Those who disobey face God's judgment; promises of blessing await the obedient. Summarize the following verses.

    Joshua 22:5

Ecclesiastes 12:13-14

Jeremiah 7:23

8. In the following verses, what promises are given to those who obey God?

    Psalm 25:10

    Psalm 103:17-18

    1 John 3:21-24

For the third time, Nehemiah's enemies plotted against him and attempted to seduce him into leaving his work, this time through a false prophet in Jerusalem. Sanballat and Tobiah hired Shemaiah—who probably was a priest, as he had access to the Temple—to lure Nehemiah into disobeying God. Pretending interest in Nehemiah's welfare, Shemaiah falsely warned him of a threat on his life and encouraged him to seek refuge in the Temple.

Shemaiah hoped to completely discredit Nehemiah and his leadership. He apparently implied that this message was from God (verse 12), but Nehemiah tested the message with the Word of God (the Law) and the task God had given him. He was immediately aware that this message was not from God. Entering the "house of God," the inner holy places of the Temple, was forbidden to all but the Levitical priests. For Nehemiah to take refuge there would have been a sin, and his leadership of the people destroyed. Even if his life were genuinely threatened, Nehemiah would not disobey God.

Nehemiah was not a coward who would run and hide, leaving the work God had assigned him. If he had done so, his workers would have quit, demoralized by the lack of leadership and fearing for their own safety. Nehemiah knew God and trusted Him in every situation.

Shemaiah was not the only person in Jerusalem trying to intimidate Nehemiah. Nehemiah did not seek personal revenge but asked God to remember in judgment his enemies—Tobiah and Sanballat, the prophetess Noadiah, and the rest of the prophets—for their opposition.

God calls His people to obedience. *This is love for God: to obey his commands. And his commands are not burdensome, for everyone born of God overcomes the world. . . . Who is it that overcomes the world? Only he who believes that Jesus is the Son of God* (1 John 5:3-5). *We know that we have come to know him if we obey his commands. The man who says, "I know him," but does not do what he commands is a liar, and the truth is not in him. But if anyone obeys his word, God's love is truly made complete in him. This is how we know we are in him: Whoever claims to live in him must walk as Jesus did* (1 John 2:3-6).

Do you know God's Son, Jesus, as your Savior? Do you have the assurance that your sins have been forgiven? Do you walk in obedience and love as Jesus did? If not, why not take time right now to confess your sins and ask God for forgiveness and begin your walk with Jesus? The reward in this life is peace, joy, love, and strength for every circumstance. At the end of this life you will receive eternal life (heaven) and a crown of righteousness as you kneel at the feet of Jesus.

Recite this week's memory verse aloud.

Work Completed

Read Nehemiah 6:15-19.

1. When was the wall completed, and how long did it take?

2. What happened when Judah's enemies heard about it?

3. It took many people carrying out their responsibilities, under the leadership of a man of God, to complete the building of the wall. They had met seemingly insurmountable obstacles, but relying on the power and protection of God and the knowledge that He had ordained the task, they met the challenge and finished the wall in 52 days. Record here other tasks completed and the person or persons in authority.

   Genesis 2:2-3

   Exodus 40:33

   Ezra 6:14-15

   John 17:4 and 19:28-30

4. (Thought question) God assigns tasks to each of His children. Do you believe God is displeased when we fail to complete the assigned task? What happens within the Body of Christ when we fail?

5. Sometimes we fail in our God-given responsibilities because we feel inadequate and the task seems overwhelming. If God gives us a job, He will also give us the wisdom and strength to perform it well until it is completed. Record these verses.

   Matthew 19:26

Ephesians 3:20

Philippians 4:13

6. What advice did David give Solomon in 1 Chronicles 28:20?

7. One of the most important tasks God has given us is to continue to grow more and more in spiritual maturity through study and meditation on His Word, daily prayer, Christian books and tapes, regular praise and worship with the Body of Christ in a local church, and courageous obedience. If we abide in Him, He will abide in us (John 15:4), teaching and admonishing and guiding us, helping us grow day by day into a deeper, more mature Christian walk. Summarize Paul's prayer found in Philippians 1:9-11 . . .

and the promise found in Philippians 1:6.

8. Summarize Paul's words in Philippians 3:14-15.

9. Read 2 Timothy 4:7 and summarize this testimony Paul wrote near the end of his life.

The job was much too difficult. Enemies of the Jews gave them unending opposition. But God's men and women, working together and using their gifts, solved difficult problems and accomplished seemingly impossible goals. With God's help, the impossible can become the possible, and the task can be satisfactorily completed.

The wall was completed . . . in fifty-two days (Nehemiah 6:15). Even though the stones were readily available, and parts of the wall may still have been standing, this amazing result could have been accomplished only with the help of God. Much of the time, half of the workers were standing guard, and the working half carried or wore their weapons. There is

reason to believe that they rested each Sabbath; Nehemiah knew and obeyed the Law (Exodus 20:8-11).

There were traitors in Jerusalem itself; nobles sworn to Tobiah because of marriage alliances were corresponding with him, betraying Nehemiah's plans to Tobiah and then trying to intimidate Nehemiah by serving as agents of propaganda for Tobiah. Both Tobiah and his son had married women of Judah. Meshullam, who was the father-in-law of Tobiah's son, was one of the workers on the wall (Nehemiah 3:30), and although we are not told that he did, would have been in a position to create more difficulties for Nehemiah. No wonder Meshullam opposed Ezra's edict for the men of Israel to separate themselves from their foreign mates (Ezra 10:10-15)!

It took a man of courage and integrity to resist the deception and threats of his enemies and keep focused on the task at hand. Nehemiah trusted his all-powerful God to help him bring about its completion.

The surrounding enemy nations realized that it could have been only by the grace of God that the work was completed so quickly despite overwhelming odds. As a result, they became fearful and lost confidence.

When you feel discouraged or inadequate, instead of letting it rob you of the joy of knowing and serving Christ, keep your eyes on Him and allow Him to help you grow daily into spiritual maturity—the maturity that will enable you to trust God as Nehemiah did. You must have a firm foundation on which to build—knowing Jesus Christ as Savior and Lord (1 Corinthians 3:11). Build with high-quality materials—time spent daily in the Word and in prayer, and faithful obedience.

Don't stay a spiritual infant; allow God to work in your life, and grow daily with His help into a more mature Christian. God won't give up on you; He will be faithful to complete the work He has begun. Fight the good fight! Finish the race! Your reward is waiting in heaven (2 Timothy 4:8).

Days 1-5 written by Helen Silvey

MEMORY CHALLENGE

"You will be called _____ of
_____ _____, _____ of
_____ with _____."

Isaiah 58:12*b*

Willing to Serve

Read Nehemiah 7:1-3.

1. What happened after the wall had been rebuilt and the doors were put in place?

2. Who was put in charge of Jerusalem and why?

3. Who were to be appointed as guards, and where were their posts to be?

4. What do you believe should be the requirements of one willing to serve God? After listing some of your own ideas, record the basic concept presented in each of the following scriptures.

   Psalm 2:11

   Psalm 101:6

   Matthew 6:24

   Acts 20:19

   Romans 12:11

   Galatians 5:13

5. What are some of the rewards of willingness to serve? For help with your answer, look up John 12:26, Romans 14:18, and Colossians 3:23-24.

Linda, a young mother, had a friend and former neighbor who was elderly and lived alone. Mrs. Brown had never had children, and her husband was now deceased. She felt somewhat isolated as she did not attend church and was not active in any other organization. She had no regular daily contact with anyone. Linda, however, went out of her way to check on and include Mrs. Brown.

As the years went by, Mrs. Brown became more isolated and unable to care for herself. Linda had been assisting her with light household chores but now found herself completely immersed in the role of caretaker. Mrs. Brown's care became an enormous part of Linda's daily activities.

Linda wasn't being paid for her service to Mrs. Brown nor was she being greatly appreciated by Mrs. Brown's relatives. She certainly wasn't hoping for an inheritance upon Mrs. Brown's death. Why was she so willing to help? The answer is found in a phrase in Nehemiah 7:2 that refers to Hanani: *He was a man of integrity and feared God more than most men do.* Linda was a woman of integrity with a fear of God and therefore was willing to serve. Her motivation for serving Mrs. Brown was not for a reward, although we can be sure the Lord will reward her. But her devotion to Mrs. Brown came out of who Linda was as a person. She would not leave Mrs. Brown alone when no one else seemed to care. She was Jesus to Mrs. Brown.

The situation with Mrs. Brown caused much stress in Linda's already-busy life. Yes, she struggled from time to time with resentment. But she persevered because of her integrity and her fear of the Lord. She beautifully demonstrated a willingness to serve.

Day 6 written by Linda Shaw

MEMORY CHALLENGE

Write out memory challenge passages for the first five lessons of Nehemiah:

Isaiah 60:18

Isaiah 58:11a-12b

Nehemiah

LESSON 6

■ A study of Nehemiah 7:4—8

Life—the Book

Read Nehemiah 7:4-73.

1. In Nehemiah 7:4, the author tells us that Jerusalem is large and spacious, but has two problems. What are they?

2. So what did God put in Nehemiah's heart to do?

3. In Nehemiah 7:5, Nehemiah made a discovery. What did he find?

4. List the categories used in the registry.

5. Do you remember a similar list of exiles in the Book of Ezra? Give the scripture reference.

6. What was the purpose of the Urim and Thummim mentioned in verse 65? You might want to use a dictionary, concordance, or the Ezra Bible study to find the answer.

7. Record the following scriptures, which help give an understanding of why being a part of the list of exiles was important.

Exodus 19:5-6

Deuteronomy 11:18-21 (Summarize)

Psalm 112:6

MEMORY CHALLENGE

Psalm 1:1

Blessed is the man who does not walk in the counsel of the wicked or stand in the way of sinners or sit in the seat of mockers.

(NIV)

Nehemiah had accomplished the rebuilding of the wall, which greatly helped to reestablish Jerusalem as a city. But the houses had not been rebuilt, nor were there enough people to populate them. Nehemiah felt led by God, therefore, to take a census in order to assess the situation concerning the repopulation process. However, it just so happened that Ezra's list of exiles, which was probably stored in the Temple archives, was discovered at this time.

If you studied Ezra, you'll remember that, for a Jew, being listed in the genealogical record was crucial. In our society we have last names such as Miller, Brown, or Smith, but in Old Testament times the genealogical record was the only proof of identity. If one's name was missing from the list, his or her only hope was to have the priest bring the Urim and Thummim, pray over the name, and then let God direct the answer. Being included on the list, and therefore proving heritage as a Jew, was vital.

There are minor differences between Ezra's and Nehemiah's lists of exiles. It's possible that Ezra's list was corrected after the people were established in Jerusalem and before the list was stored in the Temple archives. Certainly it is realistic to think that the lists would not match exactly after 14 years.

My children's paternal great-great-grandfather was a full-blooded Cherokee Indian. Therefore, they are one-sixteenth Native American, which could afford them many educational benefits in this country. In elementary schools, the federal government provides school supplies for Native American children. College students benefit because Uncle Sam provides funds for a big portion of their education. My children had only one problem. Great-great-grandpa was ashamed of his Indian blood, so he would not register his name or family with the federal government. Now my children have no way of proving their heritage. Even though blood lines could be traced back, it is too late. How I wish our government used the Urim and Thummim!

But proving Jewish heritage in Nehemiah's day or Native American heritage in our day is nothing compared to having our names written on the most important list of all time.

Then I saw a great white throne and him who was seated on it. Earth and sky fled from his presence, and there was no place for them. And I saw the dead, great and small, standing before the throne, and books were opened. <u>Another book was opened, which is the book of life.</u> The dead were judged according to what they had done as recorded in the books. The sea gave up the dead that were in it, and death and Hades gave up the dead that were in them, and each person was judged according to what he had done. Then death and Hades were thrown into the lake of fire. The lake of fire is the second death. <u>If anyone's name was not found written in the book of life, he was thrown into the lake of fire</u> (Revelation 20:11-15, emphasis added).

I did not see a temple in the city, because the Lord God Almighty and the Lamb are its temple. The city does not need the sun or the moon to shine on it, for the glory of God gives it light, and the Lamb is its lamp. The nations will walk by its light, and the kings of the earth will bring their splendor into it. On no day will its gates ever be shut, for there will be no night there. The glory and honor of the nations will be brought into it. Nothing impure will ever enter it, nor will anyone who does what is shameful or deceitful, but <u>only those whose names are written in the Lamb's book of life</u> (Revelation 21:22-27, emphasis added).

This is the list I want to have my name written on—the list in the Book of Life.

Listened Attentively

Read Nehemiah 8:1-3.

1. Who is mentioned for the first time in the Book of Nehemiah?

2. What did this man do?

3. How did the people respond?

4. God's Word admonishes us to listen or to hear. Record the following scriptures.

   Matthew 17:5

   John 5:24

   John 8:47

   Romans 10:17

   James 1:19

5. What should be the result if we listen attentively? Summarize the following scriptures to help with your answer.

   Matthew 7:24

   Matthew 13:23

   James 1:22

Have you ever been on a diet for a while and eaten nothing but healthful foods such as fruits, vegetables, fish, and lean meat? Afterward, if you indulge in a special dessert, doesn't it taste unbelievably delicious? After being deprived of such food, our taste buds become highly sensitized to sweets or fat.

The people of Jerusalem were hungry for God's Word. It was new and fresh and much needed. Having been deprived of the regular reading of the Law, they were highly sensitized to what it had to say. How else could they have stood for six hours just listening to the Scripture being read?

The story is told of a young Russian who was raiding churches after the Communist takeover. He and fellow zealots would go into a church and bring all the books out to throw in a pile for a huge bonfire. He felt that God had no place in government. But at one church, his friends noticed he was missing when the bonfire was lit. When they found him, he was weeping. As he had pulled a stack of books out of the church, one looked familiar. He had opened it and found that it was his grandmother's Bible. As a little boy he had sat in her lap as she read the Scriptures to him. That was one of his only memories as a child of a moment of true love and caring. When he found God's Word and made the connection with his grandmother, he suddenly knew he was hungry. The words made him weep.

Why do we sometimes not respond to God's Word? Maybe we are so saturated we don't even really listen. A woman dreamed she was at a party with a well-known hostess in her community. Everyone was quiet, even though the living room was packed with people. The hostess looked at the woman and said, "People never talk until they get thirsty and have something to drink." The woman woke up thinking that perhaps we should never talk until we get thirsty for God and go to Him for a drink first. In other words, we shouldn't talk until we listen to Him.

What is the art of listening? How do we listen attentively? Listening is an acquired skill that comes from the active process of trying to hear. Listening has four components: (1) receiving of information, (2) deciding to focus on what is being said, (3) understanding, and (4) remembering. Roadblocks to good listening are judgmentalism, defensiveness, not paying attention, assumptions, jumping to conclusions, and advising. Listening is hard work. It requires us to stop talking, concentrate on what is being said with an open heart and mind, and ask appropriate questions. In short, to listen attentively we have to want to hear the message, understand the message, and receive the message.

The exiles now living in Jerusalem wanted to hear and receive the Word. They listened attentively.

MEMORY CHALLENGE

Try to find a way today to encourage and bless someone who models Psalm 1:1.

Lord, Great God

Read Nehemiah 8:4-6.

1. What did Ezra do in this passage?

2. Who did Ezra praise?

3. How did the people respond?

4. Record the names for the Lord, the great God, found in the following scriptures.

   Genesis 14:22

   Genesis 17:1

   Genesis 21:33

   Psalm 91:1

   Isaiah 1:24

   Isaiah 57:15

   Matthew 6:26

   1 Timothy 1:17

In the Book of Nehemiah, Ezra is mentioned for the first time in chapter 8. He had arrived 13 years before Nehemiah and was probably much older. Ezra was the religious leader; Nehemiah was the political leader. This divided leadership between the two men was probably not threatening to the ruling government of Persia.

Where has Ezra been throughout the Book of Nehemiah? We must remember that these are probably Ne-

hemiah's memoirs. Up to this point, Ezra had not played an important enough role to mention him. He was probably in the background doing what God had instructed him to do, which was to study the Law thoroughly and to be able to present it to the people. So when the time came, Ezra was ready. He was now in the forefront leading the people in worship of the Lord, the great God.

Probably the Law could not be read to the people in a group like this until the city was secured. But when the wall was completed, a big platform was built by the Water Gate for Ezra to stand on and proclaim the Word. The Water Gate was the symbol of living water, which is God's Word. Ezra led the people in prayer, focusing on Yahweh, the Lord, the great God. First the people lifted their hands in praise, then they knelt and put their faces to the ground to show God their humility.

What an awesome experience it is to humble ourselves before God and proclaim Him Lord, the great God!
> Holy, holy, holy! Lord God Almighty!
> Early in the morning our song shall rise to Thee.
> Holy, holy, holy! merciful and mighty!
> God in three Persons, blessed Trinity!
> —Reginald Heber

5. When you praise God, what are some names you use to describe Him? Try to think of a name or description of God for each letter of the alphabet.

A—Awesome	N—
B—	O—
C—	P—
D—	Q—
E—	R—
F—	S—
G—	T—
H—	U—
I—	V—
J—	W—
K—	X—
L—	Y—
M—	Z—

MEMORY CHALLENGE

Who is blessed, according to Psalm 1:1?

Light

Read Nehemiah 8:7-8.

1. Look up Psalm 119:105 in at least two translations. Record both.

2. Which verse in today's lesson refers to the Word as "light"? Record the number of the verse, along with the key phrase.

3. Earlier this week we studied that opening our ears and listening attentively, we give God an opportunity to speak to us. Today we are emphasizing that God's Word is light and opens our vision. Summarize how each of the following verses relates to this concept.

   2 Samuel 22:29

   Psalm 27:1

   Psalm 36:9

   Proverbs 6:23

   Matthew 4:16

   Ephesians 5:8-14

4. How does the light of God's Word change us? Jot down some of your own ideas. Then record the following scriptures.

   John 12:35-36

   Romans 12:2

   1 John 2:9-10

5. (Personal) Is God's Word a light to you? When you are confused or questioning or seeking knowledge of God himself, does His Word illuminate your path? If so, take time to praise God for this influence in your life. If not, pray and ask that His Word would become a light to you.

When all the people of Jerusalem gathered at the Water Gate, Ezra probably brought the entire Pentateuch. Since he read for six straight hours, it's possible that he was able to read through a good portion of it. But one interesting part of the scripture for today's lesson concerns the Levites stationed throughout the crowd. Ezra probably read for a while, then stopped so these men could ask the people if they understood what had been said. Their job was to explain the portions of scripture Ezra read. Much like we do in the Wisdom of the Word series, the people were broken into small groups with an appointed leader. They were allowed to ask the leader anything, because the purpose was to gain understanding.

When you read the scriptures, do you just hurry through them? Or do you really read to receive understanding? When you come across a tough portion, do you wrestle with it, asking God to give you light? Is your heart set for the Word to be clear and meaningful?

God truly wants us to understand His Word. In Acts 8:26-40, an Ethiopian eunuch in charge of Queen Candace's treasury was trying to read Isaiah 53:7-8 as he traveled in his chariot. The Holy Spirit told Philip to run with the chariot and stay near it. Philip then asked, *Do you understand what you are reading?* The Ethiopian replied, *How can I . . . unless someone explains it to me?* When Philip explained it, the man received light. Through God's Word, he understood about Jesus Christ and accepted Him as his Savior.

Paul Harvey tells the story of "The Day Philip Joined the Group." In a third grade Sunday School class, the scriptures explaining the death and resurrection of Jesus had been opened to the children. One week after Easter, the teacher took the children outside in the beautiful spring air and gave each one a plastic egg. They were to find some symbol of new life, pull the egg apart, and deposit their symbol inside.

When the children had collected their items and gathered again, they all had similar things like grass, leaves, or flowers. All except Philip. Philip was a Down Syndrome child and had difficulty fitting in with the group. When he was asked to open his egg, it was empty. The children laughed, but Philip said, "I did it right. It's empty—the tomb is empty!" The class fell silent, and Philip became a part of the group that day. He had heard the Word, listened attentively, and it had become light to his soul. Then he was able to share that light with others.

Write out this week's memory challenge.

Live It Up!

Read Nehemiah 8:9-12.

1. In today's scripture, what was the people's initial reaction to the reading of the Law?

2. List all the verbs (action words) from verse 10 in Nehemiah's instructions to the people.

3. Why did Nehemiah tell the people not to weep?

4. Summarize the following scriptures that remind us that the joy of the Lord is our strength.

   Psalm 21:1

   Psalm 28:7

   Psalm 81:1

   Habakkuk 3:18-19

5. Record Jeremiah 15:16. Do you believe this is how the people felt on the day of the reading of the Law?

6. Several times in the Books of Ezra and Nehemiah we have seen how the people have been confronted with their sin and wept over it in repentance. But this time Nehemiah said, "It's time to live it up!" God is our strength, and there is joy in Him! Ask yourself two questions. What or who is your strength? From where does your joy come? Write some of your thoughts below.

As the Law was read the people wept, because they knew they had fallen short of God's expectations for their lives. But Ezra's reading of the Law made it a holy day, so Nehemiah proclaimed that all the people should be filled with joy. When we recognize our sin and repent, we, too, should be filled with joy.

Nehemiah and Ezra instructed the people to celebrate and give gifts to those in need. That was his way of making sure the poor people were able to celebrate as well. So "living it up" was not to be a time of self-service but a time of sharing. They were to have joy in the Lord as instructed in Deuteronomy 26:11, which reads, *And you and the Levites and the aliens among you shall rejoice in all the good things the LORD your God has given to you and your household.*

Joanna had not had a very happy life in the eyes of the world. Her first husband had abused their children. For the safety of the children, she boldly demanded that he leave the home. She got a full-time job, and in addition, she cleaned houses at night and on the weekends to make ends meet. Joanna kept her children in church and tried to raise them in a way pleasing to God.

Eventually she was remarried to a fine man with whom she found some security and happiness. But a few years later, he developed an inoperable brain tumor. Joanna cared for him until his death. During this time her grown children were experiencing struggles with depression, marital problems, and unemployment. But she valiantly marched on.

One Sunday evening at church, Joanna was praying with a desperate young mother at the altar. Joanna recalled her own experiences and advised the young woman, "Be joyful! We are commanded to have joy! Our only strength is in the joy of the Lord!"

That was her secret! People had wondered how she was always so cheerful and optimistic, and how she had persevered with so much tragedy in her life. The joy of the Lord was her strength! Whether rich or poor, in sickness or in health, in winter or in summer, we can "live it up" in our Heavenly Father. May your strength come from finding your joy in the Lord!

MEMORY CHALLENGE

Fill in the blanks:

"Blessed is the man who does not _____ in the
_____ of the _____ or
_____ in the way of _____ or
_____ in the seat of _____."

Psalm 1:1

Live-in Booths

Read Nehemiah 8:13-18.

1. At the beginning of the 8th chapter of Nehemiah (verse 2), what was the date?

2. According to Numbers 29:1-5, what were the people to do on this date?

3. What was the name of this feast?

4. In Nehemiah 8:14, what did the people discover they were to do during the seventh month?

5. According to Deuteronomy 16:13-15, what feast was this, and what were the instructions regarding it?

6. Look up the following scriptures to increase your knowledge of the Feast of the Tabernacles. Record the key points.

   Leviticus 23:39-43

   Deuteronomy 31:10-11

   Hosea 12:9

7. When was the last time the Feast of the Tabernacles had been celebrated like this?

8. What was the amount of the people's joy?

When I was two years old, my father was drafted into the army and stationed at a military base in

San Francisco. During that time my family developed a love for camping, because one of the most scenic places in the world, Yosemite National Park, was easily accessible. I can remember wading in the river, running from snakes, sleeping on cots in the tent, roasting marshmallows over the campfire, and seeing the famous fire fall from Yosemite Falls at night.

As an adult, I still enjoy camping. I love to be in the great outdoors and smell the clean, brisk air, build a campfire at night, and cook over a Coleman stove. I love to walk in the woods, play catch with the football, and sit in a lawn chair to read a good book. It is so refreshing to be away from telephones, television, pagers, and video games. When I have not been camping for a while, I find a great longing in my spirit to get away and linger in God's great outdoors by camping.

Certainly my love of camping stems from my childhood experience. But as I've matured, I've come to recognize another reason I enjoy it. Yes, it gets me away from modern-day technology, but it also gets me away from comfort. It gets me "back to basics." While camping, I am reduced to thinking about how to prepare a meal, build a fire, have a warm place to sleep, stay safe from little creatures and snakes, and perform basic grooming. I have to concentrate on the necessities. Then when I go back home, I really appreciate every modern convenience I have! It helps me put my life in perspective and remember how blessed I am.

I believe God may have had something similar in mind when He ordained the Feast of Booths for His people. Seven days of living in little houses made of branches was undoubtedly a great reminder of things for which they had to be thankful. Their ancestors had lived that way for 40 years in the desert trying to make it from Egypt to the Promised Land. God wanted to remind His people of that and how blessed they now were. He wanted them to remember the protection and guidance He gave during those years of wandering. They were to contemplate where they now stood in relationship to their ancestors' situation at the beginning of their journey. The purpose of celebrating the Feast of Booths was to give the people opportunity to express thankfulness.

I'm glad that, as Christians today, we don't have to celebrate those Old Testament feasts. Who would want to live in a booth for seven days? I'm thankful that this is no longer a requirement, only voluntary for those who love camping. We *are* required to have joy and to celebrate God's goodness. Remember all God has blessed you with and be thankful.

Written by Linda Shaw

Write the definition of the word "blessed." List some of the ways you have been blessed this past week.

Notes:

Nehemiah

■ A study of Nehemiah 9

Recipe for Community

Read Nehemiah 9, concentrating on verses 1-5a.

1. Nehemiah 9 is believed to chronologically follow Ezra 10. Review that chapter and record the primary sin the people were confessing.

2. What had happened in regard to this sin by the time Nehemiah 9 was written?

3. Find the verb phrases (or phrases that describe the actions of the people) in Nehemiah 9:1-5a.

4. Summarize the following scriptures for each of the topics listed.

    Obedience:
    Deuteronomy 6:18

    Psalm 106:3

    Romans 2:13

Confession:
Leviticus 26:40-42

1 John 1:9

God's Word:
2 Timothy 3:16-17

Hebrews 4:12

Worship:
1 Chronicles 16:8-10

John 4:23-24

5. Using Question 4 as a guideline, fill in the blanks for a "recipe for community."
    In Christian group combine 2 cups of _____ with the melted "stop sinning." Add a heaping table-spoon of _____. Blend "in reading from

_____ _____." Add another heaping tablespoon of _____ (hint: Nehemiah 9:3). On high temperature mix in _____, being sure to include _____ (verse 5). Cook for a day, and you have servings of community.

The Israelites had separated themselves from foreigners, which demonstrated the fact that they were turning from their sin and choosing to obey God. The reading of the Book of the Law took about three hours. Then one set of Levites led in confession for three hours, and another set led in worship. As some of the names are the same (verses 4-5), it is assumed some men were assigned to both sets. How exciting and awesome it must have been when the Levites on the stairs commanded, *Stand up and praise the Lord your God, who is from everlasting to everlasting* (Nehemiah 9:5)!

It seems that the first five verses of Nehemiah 9 give us a recipe for a right relationship with God. Four important parts are outlined for us—obedience, confession, reading and hearing God's Word, and worship and praise. These have been discussed often, but let's examine each one of these in light of "community."

The Old Testament shows a repeated pattern of God calling a community (the Israelites or Hebrews) to obedience. Each time they forsook His law, the loving Heavenly Father would send a prophet, king, or layman such as Nehemiah to call the people back to obedience. Often the people would not listen, which brought disastrous results. On one occasion, God's people spent 40 years wandering around in a wilderness; other times they were overrun by other nations and carried into captivity. When they did listen, God would restore the nation and bless them. His protection and blessings were always connected with obedience.

This need for the Christian community to obey continued into the New Testament. What happened to Ananias and Sapphira when they lied to Peter? Read Acts 5:1-11 if you do not know. In another instance, Paul admonished the Corinthians to expel an immoral member so he could repent and not contaminate their fellowship (see 1 Corinthians 5:1-5). We, too, must recognize that if we want our fellowship to be blessed, we must be obedient. God's Law does not change. To receive His protection, power, and blessings, our community needs to be one that obeys.

In Nehemiah's day, it was a common practice for people to outwardly display their grief during times of confession. They fasted and wore sackcloth, putting dust on their heads as a public sign of sorrow and repentance. The sackcloth, which was a hairy material, must have been quite uncomfortable. It represented sacrifice, and wearing it demonstrated willingness to place a higher priority on spiritual needs than on physical comfort.

The confession was intertwined with the reading of God's Word. As we really hear what the Scriptures say, we are made aware of our sins. J. Vernon McGee, the author of the "Through the Bible" commentary series, believes "confession means to agree with God's Word instead of offering excuses or attempting to rationalize our actions." The Hebrews believed that public confession helped hold them accountable.

We cannot be certain what form this public confession took. Possibly each one lifted his or her arms heavenward or knelt and bowed his or her head and confessed aloud to God. Others around were involved in their own confessions, so while public, it was also still private. Something similar takes place in many of our modern churches today when people are asked to come forward, kneel at an altar, or stand if they wish to confess Christ as their Savior. The confession is both public and private. It is a personal matter between the sinner and God, yet it holds group accountability. When we are overwhelmed by guilt, we need to remember God's mercy. When we realize that we are all simply former sinners who have been saved by grace, then we become "community."

Listening to the reading of God's Word, recognizing sin and confessing it, and turning to obedience should lead us to worship. The *Guideposts Family Concordance* defines worship as the "expression of the relationship between believers and God; involves reverence and adoration of God." Richard Foster in his book *Celebration of Discipline* states, "To worship is . . . to know, to feel, to experience the resurrected Christ in the midst of the gathered community. It is a breaking into the Shekinah (or the radiance of God dwelling in the midst of His people)." Certainly this would require praise. And as a true community, lifting our voices together to adore Christ the Lord and praising our Heavenly Father would be acts of worship. When we worship together, the Lord is pleased with His community and gives us opportunity as individuals to be encouraged.

Good community does have a recipe. If you find yourself in a community in which one or more of the necessary elements are lacking, would you ask God what He would like your part to be in correcting that now? If you belong to a community of believers in which this recipe is present, take time to thank God, for you are truly blessed.

Review

Read Nehemiah 9:5b-15.

1. What instructions were given to the Israelites by the Levites?

    As you continue reading verses 5 and 6, let your heart prayerfully praise the Lord as the Israelites did.

2. What is being described in verse 6?

3. How does Hebrews 11:3 explain how God created the universe?

4. What is the most amazing part of all of God's creation? Summarize:

    Psalm 139:13-15

    2 Corinthians 5:17

5. God kept His promise to Abraham because _____ _____ _____ (Nehemiah 9:8).

6. Name the miracles described in verses 9-12.

7. What is described in verses 13 and 14?

8. How was food and water provided?

Today's portion of scripture gives a beautiful review of God's ministry to Israel. Verse 6 extols the wondrous creativity of God. Verses 7 and 8 recall that He is the God of the covenant with Abraham. In verse 8 "the promise fulfilled" was the coming of Abraham's seed, Jesus Christ (Galatians 3:16) and the reclaiming of the Promised Land. (The boundaries of the Promised Land were given the first time in Genesis 15:18-21.)

As the people continue their confession of the goodness and mercy of God, they list the miracles that allowed them to leave Pharaoh and Egypt; then the many miracles that took them onward to fulfill God's promise of the land of Canaan.

As they considered their history, they could have compared it with the journey from their exile in Babylon to Jerusalem to rebuild the Temple and the walls. In both journeys, there were many difficulties and enemies that tried to hinder and stop their progress. But in both endeavors God was faithful to His chosen ones, and the people praised Him for His gracious care of them through several generations past.

What does this say to us for today? Is your life a journey with difficulties and enemies who want to defeat you? Like the Jewish nation that was brought out of Egypt, we have been redeemed from the world, identified with Jesus Christ, and nourished with spiritual food and drink. Instead of the pillar of cloud and fire to guide us, we have been given a map—His Word—which nourishes and guides us. God loves us unconditionally, but we cannot experience His love unless we are obedient to His will. We need never fear the *will* of God, because it comes from the *heart* of God.

Psalm 33:11 tells us, *The plans of the LORD stand firm forever, the purposes of his heart through all generations.*

The Word that created and controls the world can also perfectly control our lives. God wants to write His Word on our hearts and make it a part of our inner person (2 Corinthians 3:1-3). If we love His Word (if our *delight is in the law of the Lord*), meditate on it daily (*and on his law we meditate day and night* [Psalm 1:2]), and radically obey it, the Holy Spirit will transform our lives in such a way that in the midst of difficulties with enemies coming against us, we will have peace.

Dear Lord, may You find our hearts as faithful to You as was Abraham's (Nehemiah 9:8)!

How does the person who is blessed feel about the Law?

Rebelled, but God

Read Nehemiah 9:16-25.

1. The theme for today is Nehemiah 9:17. Record this verse word for word.

2. In this section, God's faithfulness is contrasted with the people's waywardness. Summarize the following scriptures, which show how this pattern was repeated over and over again in Israel's history.

   Rebellion
   Exodus 16:2-5, 19-20, 27-30

   Deuteronomy 31:24-27

   Judges 2:10-15

   1 Samuel 8:4-9

   But God
   Deuteronomy 2:7

   Joshua 21:43-45

   Psalm 78:23-24, 52-53

3. Record the following verses, which also reveal the character of God.

   Nehemiah 9:20

   Nehemiah 9:25

4. On your own, find one verse in the Bible that tells of God's graciousness, compassion, or love. You may use a verse you are already familiar with, or for this question only, use a reference book or Bible concordance.

5. God's example of forgiveness helps us forgive others. What does Jesus say about this in Matthew 18:21-22?

Nehemiah 9:16-25 tells us that God stood by His people. They rebelled, but God did not forsake them. Instead, He provided for their needs in the wilderness, subdued the Canaanites, and brought the Israelites into the Promised Land. All of us who know Him are former sinners who have been saved by the grace of God. All of us have rebelled, but God continues to be faithful to us.

Sam was a teenage boy in rebellion. Although raised in a loving Christian home, he chose drugs and alcohol and broke every one of his parents' rules. There were nights his mother and father did not know where he was. They only knew he did not come home. They would go out looking for him, praying they would find him safe and sound.

Sam rebelled, but God never gave up on him. A wise man once said, "You can let go of God, but God will never let go of you." This fit Sam's situation. Today, many years later, he is a pastor, having first served as a missionary. Anyone who meets Sam senses what a fine man he is, full of integrity and love for his Heavenly Father. Sam rebelled, but God in His goodness and grace never gave up or let go.

MEMORY CHALLENGE

In a Bible concordance or dictionary, look up the word "delight," and write the definition here.

Rescue— Tough Love

Read Nehemiah 9:26-27.

1. Summarize today's scripture.

2. Summarize 2 Chronicles 36:15-16.

3. Jesus told a story of a young man who rebelled. Possibly his father had repeatedly tried to bring his son back to right behavior and to God, but the son refused to listen. Finally the father made a tough decision. What was this, and what happened in the story after the father's decision? See Luke 15:11-32.

4. Were there times when God quit taking care of His people temporarily to bring them back to himself? If you can, give an example.

5. Summarize Deuteronomy 4:29-31, specifically recording verse 29.

Nehemiah 9 is a recounting of how the people rebelled repeatedly, but God rescued them again and again when they turned to Him. Yet sometimes we overlook the fact that God rarely rescued His people immediately. Usually years of sinning and disobedience would go by until the circumstances of the people became so adverse that they could tolerate it no longer. When they were lying in the bed they had made, they found out how miserable it was and cried to be rescued.

God allowed His people to suffer the consequences of their own behavior. When they chose evil, God would not intervene to protect them from that evil. He allowed them to feel the devastation of their own choices. He loved them so much that He looked not to the moment or the temporary, but to the long run or the permanent. If God immediately rescued His people from the consequences of wrong choices, they would never learn the valuable, necessary lesson of obedience. Therefore, He allowed them to suffer so that they would learn to turn to Him for rescue and begin to choose Him first.

As Christians today, we may sometimes think it is our responsibility to rescue those in rebellion before they suffer the consequences. We sometimes think it's our job to protect people from evil. But according to the pattern shown us in the Word, God always allows His people to have free choice. If we choose evil, we must suffer in order to be brought back to Him. We actually might interfere with God's plan by rescuing too soon.

When the prodigal son left home, we know his father's heart must have been heavy. He probably did not know if he would ever see his son again. Obviously the son chose a very rebellious lifestyle. The father knew the risks and had no guarantees that his son would ever return to him.

But because of the father's wisdom and courage, he was able to allow his prodigal son to hit rock bottom. Things couldn't get much worse than longing to have the pig's slop for dinner. That was the moment the son realized that the path he had chosen was one of destruction. That was the moment the son made a new choice—a choice for good and for God.

What if the father had protected the son from the consequences of his own behavior? What if he continued to send him money in that foreign country or got a friend there to take him in and let him live in his home? Would the prodigal son have hit rock bottom? No, he would have been protected from the evil of his own choice. He might have been able to go on living like that forever.

When we protect and care for someone God wants to rescue, we thwart His plan. There is often a fine line between when we should care and protect and when we should let go and let one suffer the consequences of his or her own behavior. But when we never draw the line and always care and protect, we limit God. Love is sometimes tough. We have to have enough courage and faith to let our loved ones go to the "pigpen" in order that God can make a miraculous rescue and they can come back home.

Days 1, 3, and 4 written by Linda Shaw

Try to recite the verse correctly aloud.

Returning Again to Evil

Read Nehemiah 9:28-31.

Often the blessings of God cause us to forget Him. Verse 28 tells of the repeated disobedience of the Israelites as they continue their prayer of confession.

1. Summarize verse 28 as briefly as possible.

2. Record Psalm 106:43.

3. Record Isaiah 30:18.

4. From Nehemiah 9:29 list the phrases that describe the actions of the Israelites.

5. Summarize Zechariah 7:11-12.

6. How does Nehemiah 9:30-31 describe God's faithfulness?

7. Summarize the following verses:

   2 Kings 17:13

   Psalm 78:38

   Isaiah 48:9

8. Record James 1:25.

As God's people continue in their lengthy prayer of confession, they explain that God's blessing continued in spite of their rebellion; also rebellion continued in spite of His blessing. They heard the Word of God but placed no importance on being obedient to its commandments. They saw miracles performed on their behalf but didn't respond in faith, reverence, or gratitude. They became self-indulgent, fell under the power of luxury, became totally corrupt, and sinned against all the mercies of God. He then had to destroy them by His judgments.

Some of our modern-day fallen television evangelists may have been very sincere in their commitment to God when they began, but as the last two sentences in the preceding paragraph describe the Israelites, they also describe these failed ministers. Worship of power, money, and ego, plus sexual promiscuity, finally destroyed them and many of those who followed blindly. We can see sinful nature hasn't changed them. We need to be living a devoted life for God, or we can be led astray as they were.

Nehemiah is a wonderful role model for the person described in James 1:25. Long before President Andrew Jackson said, "One man with courage is a majority," Nehemiah had already proved it. Consider a few of Nehemiah's well-known phrases:

> *The people worked with all their heart* (4:6).
> *Our God will fight for us!* (4:20).
> *I am carrying on a great project and cannot come down* (6:3).
> *Do not grieve, for the joy of the LORD is your strength* (8:10).
> *Remember me with favor, O my God* (5:19).
> *The gracious hand of my God [was] upon me* (2:18).

Because of his devotion and obedience to God, the hand of God was upon him—protecting, upholding, strengthening, and guiding. God wants to bless His obedient children. How different the Jewish history could have been!

Examine your obedience to scriptural principles. Ask God to reveal any blind spots that need to be made known. Obey God as never before. Be willing to make corrections in attitude and behavior. The resulting joy and peace will enrich your life and encourage a growing devotion to God and obedience to His Word.

MEMORY CHALLENGE

Do you feel you truly meditate and delight in the law of the Lord?

Righteous God

Read Nehemiah 9:32-38.

1. In the continuing prayer of confession, how was God addressed in verse 32?

2. Record Deuteronomy 7:9.

3. As the people continue their prayer in verse 32, what is their concern?

4. Summarize verses 33-35.

5. What are God's people confessing in Daniel 9:7-8, 14?

6. What do the people call themselves in Nehemiah 9:36?

7. Summarize Deuteronomy 28:45-48.

8. Put into your own words the distress expressed in Nehemiah 9:37.

9. What happened in verse 38?

10. Record 1 Chronicles 16:34.

11. Record phrases from these scriptures that explain the blessings of obedience.

    Exodus 23:22

    Deuteronomy 28:1

    Deuteronomy 30:2-3

12. Record phrases from these scriptures that explain how obedience compares with sacrifice.

    1 Samuel 15:22

    Psalm 50:14-15

    Micah 6:8

What is in this prayer that God did not already know? What was the point of recalling before God the all-too-well-known history of Israel's apostasy? God needed no reminder of Israel's tragic history; but in praying this way, the people were confessing to God that they understood all that had happened throughout their history. They knew that God needed to chastise His people through other nations, and they saw that He had done it with loving patience and with a purpose. Obedience to the Law was not an end in itself but an indispensable condition for the continuance of the Hebrew community.

This had at last produced the humility, repentance, and absolute trust that were essential elements in the covenant that was to be established between God and His people. They were now willing to commit themselves to a covenantal agreement.

The discipline required to be prepared to enter the covenant to keep God's laws relates to the commitment of a master gardener.

In anticipation of top-quality vegetables from his garden, the gardener begins early to develop the compost, till the soil, fertilize carefully, and select seeds from the best varieties of vegetables. He sows the seeds at the proper time and waters the soil when needed.

What would he harvest if he stopped at that point? What would happen in his carefully planned garden if he ignored the weeds, the spider mites on the tomatoes, the moles that burrow underground and eat the roots of the plants, the family dog that eats the ripe strawberries, and so much more? Is this any different from God's people neglecting their spiritual growth? We don't usually consciously make a decision to forget God—it's the neglect of the daily discipline and the gradual acceptance of the values of the world and a self-centered lifestyle that eventually replace our devotion to Him.

Every part of Scripture is God-breathed and useful one way or another—showing us truth, exposing our rebellion, correcting our mistakes, training us to live God's way. Through the Word we are put together and shaped up for the tasks God has for us (2 Timothy 3:16-17, TM).

Like the Israelites, we cannot remain devoted to our righteous God without discipline and commitment. It isn't God who neglects us. He invites His people of every generation to make new beginnings when we fail—and He lets us bury the past.

Thank You, O God, for forgiving us and remembering our past no longer.

Days 2, 5, and 6 written by Marie Coody

MEMORY CHALLENGE

Write out the entire memory verse.

Notes:

Nehemiah

LESSON 8

■ A study of Nehemiah 10—12:26

Common Folk and Kings

Read Nehemiah 10:1-27.

1. Review Nehemiah 9:38. What did the people do?

2. In addition to Nehemiah, three groups also sealed this agreement. List them. (Refer to Nehemiah 9:38 if necessary.)

3. One good reason for keeping a list of the people is found in Nehemiah 10:34 and 11:1. What is it?

4. Many lists of names are recorded in the Bible. Look up the following lists and match the scripture reference to the description of the people.

Genesis 46:8-25	People Paul greeted
2 Samuel 23:8-39	People of great faith
1 Chronicles 1:1-37	David's mighty men
Romans 16:3-16	12 tribes of Israel (Jacob's sons)
Hebrews 11	People from Adam to Abraham

5. What does Revelation 20:11-15 and 21:27 tell us about how God records the names of people?

6. Our Heavenly Father knows each one of us by name. He also knows everything concerning our relationships with other people as well as with himself. Why do you think this is important to Him? Give your reasons and back it up with scripture if possible.

7. Do you think God is still making a list of His people?

In our study of the Books of Ezra and Nehemiah, we have discovered a great many names in the recordkeeping of the people. To us this may be tedious, but to God it is important.

As we have previously learned, in Old Testament times the purpose of genealogical listings was to keep track of family lines to know which people were truly members of Israel. To be a true member, one had to be a direct descendant of one of Jacob's 12 sons who became the 12 tribes of Israel. A person's standing in the community was shown by the genealogical record.

The New Testament also contains lists. These lists generally have nothing to do with biological heritage,

Psalm 1:3

*He is like a tree
planted by streams of water,
which yields its fruit in season
and whose leaf does not wither.
Whatever he does prospers.*

(NIV)

but spiritual standing. However, in the Book of Revelation we are told of the most important record of people's names found anywhere. This record is called the Lamb's Book of Life. In this book, God keeps a list of people who have received His Son, Jesus Christ, as their personal Savior. Not only have they called Him Lord, but they have determined to live their lives by the power of His Holy Spirit. They have allowed God to convict them of their sin and deceitfulness, and they have turned from these things. They have produced good fruit in their lives by planting and watering the seeds God has given them. They are people of integrity and character who reflect the light of God's Son, Jesus.

In a certain TV commercial, a long line of people are waiting to get into heaven. A man dressed in angel garb is seated behind a desk and is naming each little sin committed by the person at the head of the line. "What about the time you hit your little sister? What about your bachelor party? What about the time you stole that notepad from work?" Somehow I don't picture heaven like this. I believe that my sins are each recorded in the Lamb's Book of Life but that the blood of Christ, my Savior, is spilled all over my page and God can no longer read my sins. They are covered by the blood! Hallelujah!

As I reviewed the lists of people recorded in Ezra and Nehemiah, I noticed very little mention of kings. God never intended for the Israelites to have a king. He planned to be their King, but they wanted to be like all the nations around them. The people came to the prophet Samuel and asked him to appoint a king. He was disturbed about this and prayed to God. *And the LORD told him: Listen to all that the people are saying to you; it is not you they have rejected, but they have rejected me as their king* (1 Samuel 8:7). So Saul was appointed king. But when he failed to keep the commands the Lord gave him, Samuel informed him, *Your kingdom will not endure; the LORD has sought out a man after his own heart and appointed him leader of his people, because you have not kept the LORD's command* (13:14). David was that king after God's own heart. He served the Lord faithfully, but his sons were evil. Soon the kingship deteriorated into one sinful king after another. Before long, the Jews were overrun by the Babylonians and carried into captivity. First, however, David was given the promise, *Your house and your kingdom will endure forever before me; your throne will be established forever* (2 Samuel 7:16).

The Restoration Period, following captivity, is what we have been studying in Ezra and Nehemiah. Ezra restored the Temple, and Nehemiah restored the wall and the city of Jerusalem, but God never restored the kingship. As you may have noticed, there have been priests and governors to lead, but no kings. The Book of Nehemiah is the last biblical chronological information we have of Israel before the New Testament begins. Did the Jews have a king in the New Testament? No, they were under the government of Rome as an occupied country. Therefore, they couldn't have had a king.

It's understandable that the Jews in Jesus' day were looking for an earthly king. The golden day of Israel was with David in all of his glory. The people once again wanted to be independent and rule themselves. They felt their only hope was for God to deliver them by giving them a king who could overthrow Rome and once again give them their own power. It's no wonder that many of them believed the Messiah would come and do just that.

But God never varied from His original idea to be their king himself. So He sent His Son to rule in His stead. His Son would be king through the line of David, to whom He had promised an everlasting kingdom. But once again God and His Son were rejected by the people. They hung His Son on a wooden cross and crucified Him. It seems that God and Israel were always at differing purposes where kingship was concerned.

However, we know this did not mean that kingship was taken from Jesus. He is still King of Kings and will rule forever and ever. *Hallelujah! For our Lord God Almighty reigns. Let us rejoice and be glad and give him glory!* (Revelation 19:6-7). *I saw heaven standing open and there before me was a white horse, whose rider is called Faithful and True. With justice he judges and makes war. His eyes are like blazing fire, and on his head are many crowns. He has a name written on him that no one knows but he himself. He is dressed in a robe dipped in blood, and his name is the Word of God. The armies of heaven were following him, riding on white horses and dressed in fine linen, white and clean. Out of his mouth comes a sharp sword with which to strike down the nations. "He will rule them with an iron scepter." He treads the winepress of the fury of the wrath of God Almighty. On his robe and on his thigh he has this name written:* KING OF KINGS AND LORD OF LORDS (verses 11-16).

Kings were largely missing from the lists of people because God intended Christ to be our king. As we accept Him as Lord and King, even though we are common folk, we find our names written in the Lamb's Book of Life. Kings are no more precious to Him than we are. May we each find our priority to be listed in the Book with all of God's people.

Curse and Oath

Read Nehemiah 10:28-39, concentrating on verses 28-31a.

1. With what did the people bind themselves?

2. What did the people promise God in verse 29?

3. According to Deuteronomy 28:9-11, what did God promise to do for His people if they would obey Him?

4. Summarize Deuteronomy 28:15-68.

5. The curse and oath basically relate to three different categories. Title them below, using these verses as hints.

   Nehemiah 10:30
   Nehemiah 10:31
   Nehemiah 10:32-39

6. List the reasons intermarriage was forbidden using Genesis 31:19, 30-32; Exodus 34:16; and Deuteronomy 7:1-6 to help you with your answer.

7. Why do you believe God did not want His people to buy or sell on the Sabbath? Look up Exodus 23:12 and Jeremiah 17:19-27 for hints.

In Deuteronomy 8, God admonished Moses to be careful to follow all of His commands. Moses was reminded that obedience would bring blessings and disobedience would bring a curse. The chapter ends, *If you ever forget the LORD your God and follow other gods and worship and bow down to them, I testify against you today that you will surely be destroyed. Like the nations the LORD destroyed before you, so you will be destroyed for not obeying the LORD your God* (verse 19).

What a choice—blessings or a curse! Obviously we hope for God's blessing on our lives. However, if we don't walk with the Lord daily and stay sensitive to His voice, we can easily get off track. This seemed to be the problem with the Israelites. They would drift. Slowly but surely they would begin to take God's laws lightly and sin would creep back in. Soon they were involved in blatant disobedience, and they would have to suffer the consequences of the curse.

When Nehemiah restored the wall, he recalled God's instruction to Moses. He knew that if the people were not careful to obey, they would be cursed. So he challenged them to take an oath that if they did not obey, they would accept the curse of God. Nehemiah was hoping this would help the people be more aware of their choices.

The agreement related to intermarriage, the Sabbath, and material resources. Intermarriage was forbidden because of the temptation to worship other gods, and also because it caused dissension within families. Consider the situation in Genesis 31 concerning Jacob and Rachel. Jacob wanted his family to have nothing to do with idols, but apparently Rachel did not have the same convictions.

The second part of the agreement involved keeping the Sabbath holy. Of course, God ordained the seventh day to be one of rest. But He also knew that if He did not specifically set aside a day for worship, people would be tempted to forget it. Time for worship would be squeezed out by the cares of the world.

Finally, buying and selling on the Sabbath was a question of who or what the people loved more—God or money. If the Israelites refused to buy and sell on the seventh day, they were putting God above money. They were willing to go one day without a profit in order to put God first. This told Him about the condition of their hearts. *For where your treasure is, there your heart will be also* (Matthew 6:21).

The choice is still before us today. There is promise of blessings or a curse according to our willingness to obey. The curse is not represented by difficult circumstances in our lives, for those will come to all of us. The curse is the long-term conclusion of separation from God. May we be wise enough to choose obedience and therefore receive eternal blessings!

MEMORY CHALLENGE

Read this week's verse several times to become familiar with it.

Covenant

Read Nehemiah 10:31b-36.

1. In your own words write a definition of "covenant." If necessary, feel free to check yourself with a dictionary or Bible concordance.

2. Other godly leaders had encouraged the people to make covenants. Summarize 2 Chronicles 34:29-31.

3. Yesterday we studied the first two parts of the covenant that dealt with intermarriage and keeping the Sabbath. Consult Nehemiah 10:31-39 to list other parts of the covenant.

4. Why were the people to forego working the land and to cancel all debts every seventh year? See Exodus 23:10 and Deuteronomy 15:1-3.

5. (Thought question) Where did Nehemiah get the idea the people should give a third of a shekel each year? In Exodus 30:11-13, Moses required half of a shekel. Why do you think Nehemiah lowered the amount?

6. Summarize Exodus 13:1-2 and Deuteronomy 26:1-2 to explain what the firstfruits are.

Over the course of many years, Ezra and Nehemiah rebuilt the Temple, the wall, and the city of Jerusalem. Now Nehemiah is trying to reinstate the laws of God by making a covenant among His people to obey. They will receive a curse if they disobey and a blessing if they obey. This covenant sounds like a promise one way or the other.

See, I set before you today life and prosperity, death and destruction. For I command you today to love the LORD your God, to walk in his ways, and to keep his commands, decrees and laws; then you will live and increase, and the LORD your God will bless you in the land you are entering to possess. But if your heart turns away and you are not obedient, and if you are drawn away to bow down to other gods and worship them, I declare to you this day that you will certainly be destroyed (Deuteronomy 30:15-18). Carefully follow the terms of this covenant, so that you may prosper in everything you do (29:9). Now that you know these things, you will be blessed if you do them (John 13:17).

Two young women each made a covenant with the Lord regarding their children. One was watching her two little girls play outside one day when God asked her to give Him her children. She said, "Yes, Lord, whatever happens, I will always give you my girls." The other was called to a mission field far away where she knew her family would not have easy access to medical care. She battled with God because He asked such a thing of her, but in time she was able to surrender her children as well.

Within a short time, the first young mother discovered that her husband had been unfaithful to her. He wanted a divorce and was unwilling to attempt to work out their relationship. She was left as a single parent to rear the girls alone. But she remained true to her covenant to give her girls to God. Through many difficult hardships, He never left her side. She eventually remarried and saw her girls grow into adulthood. They both married fine Christian men and became godly, hardworking women.

Living in a remote area, the missionary mother also endured many hardships. But God honored her covenant and her ministry. She saw her four children through to healthy adulthood. One became a pastor, another a doctor, one a missionary, and the last a layperson on the mission field. Looking back, the woman could not imagine a better life.

When we agree with God to obey Him and do whatever He asks of us, He will honor us and bring us peace and contentment. His covenant will never be void. God always makes good on His agreements.

MEMORY CHALLENGE

Who is like a tree planted by streams of water, yielding its fruit in season?

Contract to Tithe

Read Nehemiah 10:37-39.

1. In a word, what is the main idea presented in the verses for today?

2. For some background on tithing, summarize the following scriptures.

   Leviticus 27:30-33

   Deuteronomy 12:6-7

   Deuteronomy 14:22-28

3. Were the Levites also supposed to give a tithe? See Numbers 18:26.

4. What was the amount set for the tithe?

5. Did the Lord still require tithing in the New Testament? Summarize 1 Corinthians 16:2.

6. Malachi 3:10 holds a promise regarding our faithfulness in bringing God His tithe. Personalize this verse as you record it.

7. Part of the discipline of tithing concerns our readiness to give God what is His and to trust Him with our treasures. Record the following verses.

Proverbs 11:24-25

Matthew 6:20-21

The Law required one-tenth of the Israelites' produce to be taken to the Temple to support the Levites. The Levites cared for the Temple and organized all the religious observances. That was their job, and they deserved to be paid for it. But they, too, were to give a tenth of what they received to the priests so that they, too, were tithing. By following this principle, they were able to secure support for God's house and His servants. All were to make a contract to tithe.

Two friends grew up in Christian homes where both parents tithed. One family's finances were tight, and they didn't require their son to tithe his income because the money was always needed for clothes or gas or a little fun. Later, a college bill really put the son in financial distress. The family made excuses, believing their son was exempt from tithing because he didn't have much money.

The other family taught their son to tithe no matter what. From the time he was a child and began to receive an allowance, he was given three envelopes. One was for his own spending money, one was for savings, and one was for tithe. There were no excuses. The tithe came first and then he learned to manage the remaining resources.

As the two young men grew into adults, the son who was taught to tithe continued to do so. After securing his own full-time job, marrying, and having children, he found at times that money was very tight and it would be tempting to keep his tithe. But he never wavered. He always gave God His portion first.

The other son continued to use excuses. He never felt he had enough money to tithe, so he didn't. He had difficulty handling his money and making ends meet. Truthfully, he wasn't a big spender nor did he spend money foolishly, but he just could never seem to get on a budget and make it work.

When both had been married about 25 years, the tither was comfortable. He was not rich, but his needs were met and he was able to afford a few luxuries. He was content with his financial standing. He had planned for the future by setting up a college fund for his children and a retirement fund for himself and his wife. He had been faithful to God, and God had been faithful to him.

The son who never tithed still had financial problems. Each month he struggled to pay his bills. Although he had a good job, his wife and children were frustrated that there was never any money except for the basics and often they had to scrimp on those. Over the years he had depended on his parents and his wife's parents to help him buy basic furnishings for the home. This was embarrassing to him and made him feel inadequate. His retirement plans were poor, and there was no money set aside for his children's education.

We would be assuming a great deal to say this all happened because one man tithed and one man didn't. But the principle is that God requires the obedience of our hearts, including our tithe. The tithing son determined to follow God no matter what. The son who did not tithe was lax concerning many of God's laws. He didn't believe that radical obedience was important, and his parents continued to make excuses for him. Whether the blessings came to one for tithing and obedience, while problems came for the other for not tithing and disobedience, we cannot say. But certainly the scriptures for today point to blessings for obedience and problems for disobedience.

Many people in the church today have become lax regarding tithing. Maybe this lesson is just for you today. Open your heart to the Holy Spirit, and let Him lead you. If He is asking you to make a contract to tithe, be obedient and expect His blessing!

MEMORY CHALLENGE

Can you recite this week's scripture from memory yet?

DAY FIVE

City

Read Nehemiah 11:1-36.

1. Who were the main groups of people who had settled in Jerusalem? Include information from 1 Chronicles 9:2 in your answer.

2. How was it determined who else would live there?

3. Why were people needed to live in Jerusalem? (Hint: Refer to Nehemiah 7:4.)

4. Jerusalem was the Holy City and had some prophecies connected with it. Summarize the following scriptures.

   Zechariah 1:14-17

   Zechariah 8:1-8

   Revelation 21:1-4, 9-27

When the exiles returned to Israel, very few settled in Jerusalem because the town was in such disrepair and therefore vulnerable to attack. Primarily, those who were living in the city were princes or priests. The population of the city was approximately 3,000. Compared to the original population of Jerusalem, this was a small group. Large areas of the city were vacant. Since Nehemiah and his colleagues rebuilt the wall in the same place as the original wall, the area of the city was too large for the small population. In order to fill up the city, Nehemiah had to draft people by casting lots.

Why wouldn't people want to move into Jerusalem? First, non-Jews were prejudiced against those who lived in the Holy City because of their religious beliefs. Sometimes they were excluded from trade. Second, if a Jew were to move to the city, he would have to rebuild a home and reestablish a business there. This would be a great deal of work, and many were not willing to put forth the effort. Finally, there was a higher standard for obeying the law in Jerusalem near the Temple. Some Jews were not this dedicated. So in short, moving to the city was not necessarily a popular thing to do.

Nehemiah 11 centers on the city and lists the inhabitants by family heads. Those living outside Jerusalem are listed in chapter 11 according to villages.

We can't study Jerusalem without thinking of the holy city to come. Revelation 21 and 22 are full of promises concerning what our future lives will include if we are faithful to God. One of the promises concerns the new Jerusalem in heaven, where we will be allowed to dwell. The city will be laid out as a square—1,400 miles long and wide. The wall of the city will be glorious, for it will be 200 feet high and made of jasper. Each foundation will be decorated with 12 precious jewels and each of the 12 gates will be formed from a single pearl. The streets will be made of gold and the River of the Water of Life will flow from the throne of God down the middle of the city. It will be as clear as crystal, and on each side of it will stand the Tree of Life, bearing 12 crops of fruit, yielding its fruit every month.

The city will need no sun because the Lamb of God, Jesus Christ, will be its lamp and the glory of God its light. Night will have passed away, for there will be only day. The dwelling of God will be with His children. No longer will there be any curse. God will wipe away every tear, and nothing sad or painful will be there. Death will be no longer—only rejoicing. God's people will live and reign there with Him forever.

We live in a fallen world and are subject to the trials and temptations of life. But let's never forget that one day all our hardships and difficulties will pass away, for God does promise us a final reward. We can look forward to heaven! We can look forward to seeing our loved ones again! It will be glorious! The New Jerusalem will surpass any expectations we have of a marvelous city. Jesus himself will be there to meet us and live with us forever and ever!

MEMORY CHALLENGE

Describe the man from Psalm 1:3.

Christ, Our High Priest

Read Nehemiah 12:1-26 and Malachi 2:1-9.

1. What will happen to the priests if they do not listen to God and set their hearts to honor His name?

2. What will happen to the descendants of the priests?

3. According to Malachi 2:4-5, with whom did God make a covenant?

4. What was this covenant?

5. What should the lips of a priest do? What had the lips of the priests done instead?

6. What were the priests like in Jesus' day? Use Matthew 16:21; 21:14-16; and 26:63-68 to help with your answer.

7. Who is our High Priest? Summarize the following scriptures.

   Hebrews 2:17

   Hebrews 4:14-16

   Hebrews 7:22-28

   Hebrews 10:11-12

Like all human institutions, the priesthood was not always perfect. There were problems from the very beginning concerning the first priest, Aaron. In Exodus

32 the people were impatient that Moses was taking so long to meet with God on Mount Sinai. They asked Aaron to make them some gods and he immediately complied by saying, "Bring me your gold jewelry." He proceeded to make the jewels into a golden calf, which the people then worshiped. Despite his disobedience, God remained faithful to Aaron's family line.

Another example of problems in the priesthood concerns Eli. Eli was the priest with whom Hannah left her precious son, Samuel. Even though Eli was a godly man and good mentor for Samuel, 1 Samuel 2:12 tells us, *Eli's sons were wicked men; they had no regard for the Lord. These sons became the priests.*

The coming of Jesus signified the end of the priesthood. Just as He became the final sacrifice for our sins, He became the High Priest of God. With Christ there is no concern of corruption, idolatry, or dishonesty. He is truly the "authorized minister" who "mediates between God and man" *(Guideposts Family Concordance).* We no longer need to go through an earthly priest in the line of Aaron, but through Christ we have direct access to the Father. He is the sacrifice for our sins and the mouthpiece for our prayers. He is the advocate for each one of us before the Almighty God, interceding night and day. What a relief to know we have one we can totally trust to be our priest, for He is not a human priest but the Son of God. He will never let us down to look after His own interests. *We are Jesus' number one interest!*

Written by Linda Shaw

MEMORY CHALLENGE

Psalm 1:1-3:

"Blessed is the _____ who does not _____ in the _____ of the wicked or stand in the way of _____ or sit in the seat of _____. But his _____ is in the law of the Lord, and on his law he _____ day and night. He is like a _____ planted by _____ of water, which yields its _____ in season and whose _____ does not wither. Whatever he does _____."

Notes:

Nehemiah

■ **A study of Nehemiah 12:27—13:5**

DAY ONE

Preparation for Dedication

Read Nehemiah 12:27-29.

Preparations for the dedication of the walls of Jerusalem had begun. The Israelites had experienced a great deal of fear and trembling as they built the walls of Jerusalem. In our study today, we learn of their great joy and triumph as they begin to celebrate the wall's completion.

1. In verse 27, who was being brought to Jerusalem for the celebration?

2. What was their assignment?

3. 1 Chronicles 15:16 records why they were chosen for this responsibility. Explain.

4. Others were brought to Jerusalem for the celebration. Who were they, and where did they live?

5. Record Psalm 126:5.

6. Music was important throughout the Bible. Summarize these verses:

   1 Samuel 10:5

   2 Samuel 6:5

   Psalm 30:4

   Psalm 47:6

Music, both vocal and instrumental, was an important part of the festive and religious services of the Hebrews. The expression of the full range of human emotions through music was as much a part of the lives of biblical people as it is for us today.

■ In celebrating the victory of the Israelites over Pharaoh and his army (after crossing the Red Sea on dry land):
  Miriam sang to them: "Sing to the LORD, for he is highly exalted. The horse and its rider he has hurled into the sea" (Exodus 15:21).

■ In public celebrations:
  When the men were returning home after David had killed the Philistine, the women came out

MEMORY CHALLENGE

Psalm 1:5

Therefore the wicked will not stand in the judgment, nor sinners in the assembly of the righteous.

(NIV)

from all the towns of Israel to meet King Saul with singing and dancing, with joyful songs and with tambourines and lutes (1 Samuel 18:6).

■ In annual pilgrimages to Jerusalem:
You will sing as on the night you celebrate a holy festival; your hearts will rejoice as when people go up with flutes to the mountain of the LORD, to the Rock of Israel (Isaiah 30:29).

■ In martial affairs:
Jehoshaphat appointed men to sing to the LORD and to praise him for the splendor of his holiness as they went out at the head of the army, saying: "Give thanks to the LORD, for his love endures forever" (2 Chronicles 20:21).

■ In times of sorrow (while the Israelites were in captivity):
By the rivers of Babylon we sat and wept when we remembered Zion. There on the poplars we hung our harps (Psalm 137:1-2).

But it was in religious services that Hebrew music found its greatest importance. In accordance with David's plan for perfecting sacred choristry, the sons of Asaph were set apart for musical service. This royal direction of sacred music was continued during the reigns of David and Solomon with the erection of the Temple, giving it its greatest privilege of public worship and praise. Under succeeding kings it fell into partial disuse and, of course, was largely discontinued during the time of captivity. Yet the musical spirit of the Hebrews survived even this difficult time, for among the captives who returned to the Holy Land with Ezra were 200 musicians and singers to form the choirs for the dedication of the wall (Nehemiah 12:27-29).

Just as Nehemiah, when we have an occasion for celebration, many times we begin by forming an agenda that includes music. If you sing or play an instrument, you can relate to the thrill that the Israelite musicians must have experienced. To gain understanding of their worshipful excitement, imagine the choirs singing "The Hallelujah Chorus" from Handel's *Messiah* with all the instruments lifting the melody heavenward during the march on the walls.

Today music plays a vital role in our celebrations and also helps heal our hearts during times of sorrow.
- The Thanksgiving and Christmas holiday seasons provide wonderful times of singing hymns and carols that express our feelings of gratitude and love.
- During the Olympic award ceremonies, the playing of the gold medal winner's national anthem often brings tears of joy.
- All branches of our military have bands and choirs that participate in many ceremonies of our nation.

After the 1995 bombing of the Murrah Federal Building in Oklahoma City when 168 men, women, and children were killed, the wife of the governor of Oklahoma planned a memorial service for all the families and the rescue teams in order to bring comfort with words and music.

From the the winter 1996 special memorial issue of *Oklahoma Today* magazine:
The idea was conceived before the clock struck 12:00 on April 19, 1995, by First Lady Cathy Keating and a few aides and family members. Not one of them doubted that their fellow Oklahomans would come—the naked need was obvious by looking into the eyes of any Oklahoman. What no one expected was the nation to show up as well.

They drove in from Colorado, New Mexico and Texas. They flew in from New York, Washington, D.C., and points in-between (the first lady of Illinois, Brenda Edgars, sent 600 teddy bears for the bereaved families). Some arrived before dawn; by noon, radio stations broadcasted gentle warnings cautioning people that if they were not already in line, they most likely could not get in. At three o'clock in the afternoon when the doors opened, 19,000 were waiting, and still they came.

Tens of thousands of people filled first the State Fair Arena, then the Made in Oklahoma Building, and finally All Sports Stadium. Yet even more Americans eavesdropped over car radios or watched the finale—Ernestine Dillard's rendition of "God Bless America"—at home. Against a backdrop of songs, prayers, and poetry, the nation took a collective moment to share its grief and to gain encouragement from the words of Billy Graham. The day was April 25, 1995, and the death toll stood at 73 dead, 154 unaccounted for, and at least 460 injured. There was worse to come, but there was also, finally, some comfort.

Purification for Celebration

Read Nehemiah 12:30.

1. What had the priests and Levites done in preparation for the dedication of the wall of Jerusalem?

   Harper's Bible Dictionary defines "purity" as "freedom from avoidable and unavoidable contamination."

An indispensable part of the dedication was the preliminary purification of the structure and of the participants in the ceremony. Those who had been occupied with secular affairs were regarded as ritually unclean and unfit to participate in the ceremony. Priests were always purified before the ceremonies (Ezra 6:20), and laypersons also had to be pure before joining the ritual (Genesis 35:2-3). The purification was accomplished by washing, bathing, fasting, or by sprinkling with holy water or the blood of the sacrifice (Leviticus 14).

2. Read Exodus 19:9-11. What did the Lord command Moses to do?

3. Read Exodus 19:14. How did Moses and the people respond to God's command?

4. Read Numbers 19:20. What was the result if a person did not obey the purification ordinance?

Israel was God's chosen people. Their land was His holy land. Anything that made people unclean caused them to be unfit to approach God and His dwelling place. Hebrews regarded sin as defilement, which had to be cleansed or atoned for by such rites as were specified for the Day of Atonement (Yom Kippur) in Leviticus 16.

5. To familiarize yourself with the ritual of purification, scan Leviticus 16. You will feel exhausted after imagining yourself performing all of these rites!

Jesus denounced the purification rites of the priests and Pharisees, which in His day had become hopelessly burdensome. When they questioned Him about not washing His hands before eating, He explained that a person is not defiled by what enters into him or her, but by evil thoughts and motives that proceed out of the person's heart (Mark 7:18-23). He denounced those Pharisees who washed the outside of their cups and plates but failed to cleanse the inside of their filthy hearts (Luke 11:39) and told His disciples that all things were clean to them (verse 41). Jesus abolished ceremonial purifications. He told His disciples at the Last Supper, *Now ye are clean through the word which I have spoken unto you* (John 15:3, KJV). He summarized His whole teaching concerning purity by saying, *Blessed are the pure in heart: for they will see God* (Matthew 5:8).

6. (Challenge question) Below is an interesting comparison of the systems of purification, or cleansing, between the old and new covenants. Anyone who chooses to can search the scriptures for these comparisons. Use phrases from the verses that validate the claims given:

The Old Testament System	The New Testament System
Was temporary (Hebrews 8:13)	Is permanent (Hebrews 7:21)
Aaron, first high priest (Leviticus 8:2)	Jesus, only High Priest (Hebrews 4:14)
From tribe of Levi (Hebrews 7:5)	From the tribe of Judah (Hebrews 7:14)
Ministered on earth (Hebrews 8:4)	Ministers in heaven (Hebrews 8:1-2)
Used blood of animals (Leviticus 22:19)	Uses blood of Christ (Hebrews 9:12)
Required careful approach to tabernacle (Leviticus 16:2)	Encourages confident approach to throne (Hebrews 4:16)

Prayerfully thank Jesus for what He has done for you by His suffering and death.

MEMORY CHALLENGE

Who will not stand in the Judgment?

Procession of Thanksgiving

Read Nehemiah 12:31-42a.

The ceremonies of purification had concentrated on the removal of harmful impurities incurred from the past. Since the purification rites had been completed, the dedication of the wall could take place. That would ensure God's protection for the future.

1. Where did Nehemiah direct the leaders (princes) to go during the procession?

2. Who went with them and what were they doing?

3. What does verse 40 tell us about the choirs?

Nehemiah and all the Israelites were thankful to God for His protection and guidance during the completion of the repair of the wall of Jerusalem.

Part of the ritual of dedication was the procession of thanksgiving along the walls of Jerusalem. The place of assembly was in the southwest corner of the city, near the Valley Gate. That was apparently a center of activity during the time of Nehemiah's leadership. From there, each of the two groups involved moved in opposite directions, covering approximately half of the circumference of the wall. The groups were apparently identical in form, symmetrically arranged. In each group a choir was followed by a high secular official leading half of the lay leaders, followed by a group of seven priests and then eight Levites. With the vocal music from the front of the procession (Psalm 68:25) and instrumental music from the rear, the whole procession must have had stereophonic sound!

After completing their march on the wall, the two companies seem to have met at the broad place before the Water Gate (verse 37; 8:1) and from there entered the Temple to offer their sacrifices.

4. Refer back to lesson 2, page 8. Find the drawing of the gates and walls of Jerusalem. From the Valley Gate and following opposite directions, you will see the route of each choir.

Use the scriptures listed to answer the next three questions:

5. **Why** should we give thanks to God?

    Psalm 105:1

    1 Chronicles 16:34

    1 Corinthians 15:57

    2 Corinthians 9:15

6. **How** should we show we are thankful?

    Psalm 100:4

    Psalm 116:17

    Psalm 147:7

    Colossians 3:16

7. **When** should we give thanks to the Lord?

    Psalm 92:2

    Luke 9:16

    1 Thessalonians 5:18

    1 Timothy 4:4

8. Nehemiah's choirs sang songs of thankfulness. Can you think of a song that expresses your thanks to the Lord? Sing it to Him now.

MEMORY CHALLENGE

Who will not be in the assembly of the righteous?

Participation in Joy

Read Nehemiah 12:42b-43.

The two choirs that were giving thanks proceeded to the Temple of God where they took their places. They played and sang loudly and clearly.

1. Who was their choir director?

2. How did the people (including the women and children) respond on this day of celebration and dedication?

3. How were others made aware of the joy of the people?

4. The tremendous joy of other occasions is recorded in these verses. Summarize the following scriptures:

   2 Chronicles 20:27

   Ezra 6:22

5. 1 Chronicles 16:8-9 describes what was happening on this day of celebration. Record these verses.

Nehemiah's vision of restoring the walls of Jerusalem was challenged many times by his enemies. They said it could not be done, and they tried to intimidate the people involved. By commitment and perseverance, the leaders and the people proved they could solve huge problems and accomplish great goals if they were doing what God wanted them to do.

The work had been done, and now it was time to celebrate. The people remembered and honored God by worshiping and celebrating with thanksgiving and praise. The many sacrifices by which this day was marked were thank offerings in which the choicest part, the fat, was offered to God. A part was given to the priests, and the rest of the sacrificial offering was eaten by the worshiper and his family in a joyful celebration. Just as it was at the celebration in Jerusalem, the end result of all celebrations should be joy—the joy that comes from a full and grateful heart.

When we know the joy that comes from God, we don't need continual celebrations to keep us joyful. We have an inner joy, and we know that no matter what happens, God offers hope and promise.

6. Fill in the blanks:
   Do not grieve, for the _____ of the LORD is your strength (Nehemiah 8:10).
   Weeping may remain for a night, but _____ comes in the morning (Psalm 30:5).
   Tell of his works with songs of _____ (Psalm 107:22).
   When justice is done, it brings _____ to the righteous (Proverbs 21:15).

The presence of the Holy Spirit in our lives produces joy. The flood of divine joy that comes to the one who totally commits to the will of God has a marked effect upon the lives of others. It will leave its impression upon hearts throughout eternity.

As a Sunday School teacher, Mrs. Roy Cantrell was a vital influence in my life. I had never known anyone who radiated so meaningfully the truth of Galatians 5:22, which reads, *When the Holy Spirit controls our lives he will produce this kind of fruit in us: love, joy, peace, patience, kindness, goodness, faithfulness, gentleness, and self-control* (TLB). Sunday after Sunday, the delight of God's love and joy was evident in my teacher's life. Joy was the quality that was so compelling to me. For the first time I saw a life that made me want to be a Christian. The compelling quality of joy seemed to be lacking in others around me who stressed obedience to the "traditions of men." Mark 7:8 tells us, *You have let go of the commands of God and are holding on to the traditions of men.* Man-made rules quench and grieve the Holy Spirit in the hearts of believers. The Holy Spirit was faithful to convict me of my sins and to draw me to live my life in Him.

7. Ask the Lord to bring to remembrance someone who influenced you to give your life to Him. What was there about him or her that attracted you? Ask Him to show you if you need to develop a particular quality in your life so that you can be a greater influence for Him.

   Daniel 12:3—*Those who are wise will shine like the brightness of the heavens, and those who lead many to righteousness, like the stars for ever and ever.*

MEMORY CHALLENGE

Read the memory challenge until you picture in your heart what will happen to the wicked in the Judgment.

Presentation of Contributions

Read Nehemiah 12:44-47.

1. Why were the storerooms needed?

2. Where did the people get their portion of tithe to bring to the storerooms?

3. List the four groups of people in this passage of scripture who received daily portions from the storerooms.

4. Read Numbers 18:21 and record how the tithes were to be used.

5. Nehemiah 12:47 tells us that the Levites tithed to the descendants of Aaron. Summarize Numbers 18:25-28 to give more explanation.

According to scripture, we do receive blessing from giving. Fill in the blanks:

He who gives to the _____ will lack _____ (Proverbs 28:27).

Cast your _____ upon the _____, for after many days you will _____ it again (Ecclesiastes 11:1).

And if _____ gives even a cup of cold _____ . . . he will certainly not _____ his reward (Matthew 10:42).

Give, and it _____ _____ _____ to you (Luke 6:38).

It is more _____ to _____ than to _____ (Acts 20:35).

2 Corinthians 9:7 tells us, *Each man should give what he has decided in his heart to give, not reluctantly or under compulsion, for God loves a cheerful giver.*

Christians give their lives—all they are and all they have—to the Lord. When considering giving, according to 2 Corinthians 9:7, find out what satisfies your heart in God's sight, and then give it joyously. God wants us to give in faith in answer to His voice.

When we know that a gift has been given to us that was purchased out of obligation without any pleasure, how do we feel? We probably want to hand it back to the giver. But if we knew that someone was very excited to select just the right gift for us, no matter how small, we would receive it enthusiastically—and would look for an opportunity to give something in return. That is how God feels about our gifts to Him.

In His Word, God has given us guidelines for our giving. Record from each scripture reference the portion that is applicable to giving:

According to income (Deuteronomy 16:17)

Without others knowing (Matthew 6:3)

Generously (Romans 12:8)

Regularly, every week (1 Corinthians 16:2)

Cheerfully (2 Corinthians 9:7)

Are you following the guidelines? Is there one that is difficult for you? If you feel comfortable doing so, share with your group an experience you have had concerning one of the guidelines for giving. As you make a commitment to the Lord to become obedient to His Word, He will strengthen you and bless you, as only He can, for your radical obedience.

MEMORY CHALLENGE

Practice saying the memory verse aloud.

Paralyzing Fear

Read Nehemiah 13:1-3.

1. What did Nehemiah and the people learn from reading the Book of Moses?

2. Summarize Deuteronomy 23:3-6.

3. Read Numbers 22, concentrating on verses 1-14. Instead of letting the Israelites pass through their country on their way to the Promised Land, what did Balak, King of Moab, do?

4. What happened when the people heard the Law from the Book of Moses?

5. Israel, frustrated in her attempt to enter Canaan from the south, determined after years of delay to gain entry from the east through the plains of Moab. Was Balaam's time in Moab a blessing or a curse for the Moabites? Summarize the following verses for the answer:

   Numbers 31:15-18

   2 Peter 2:15

   Revelation 2:14

Experiencing fear is normal, but to be paralyzed by fear is an indication that we question God's ability to take care of His own.

6. Balak would have been wiser to have claimed the promises of these "fear not" scriptures. Record the phrase after "fear not" (or "Do not be afraid") in these verses:

   Blessings of life (Genesis 26:24)

   Needs supplied (1 Kings 17:13-14)

   Protection (2 Kings 6:16)

   Strength in weakness (Isaiah 41:10)

   Never alone in trials (Isaiah 43:1-3a)

   Forever alive (Revelation 1:17-18)

When fear strikes and you refuse to succumb to it, but instead remain calm and face it with confident faith and hope, out of it will come the ability to trust God as never before. It will bring inexpressibly wonderful peace and joy.

Like Balak, much of our fear is caused by our overreaction when we build up events in our minds and then panic over what could go wrong. When facing a seemingly impossible situation, we should do what we know is right and ask the Lord to do the rest or guide us to the solution. He may see fit to make the impossible happen. Nothing is impossible with God! He does the impossible every day!

We must ultimately come to the place in our spiritual walk at which we realize that our fearful praying must stop and a step of faith must be taken. Faith is a mind-set that expects God to act. While we are fearing that God is not answering, He is faithfully working out His purposes.

Will you take a step of faith today? After you know you have been obedient to biblical principles in your situation, release it to the Lord and let Him do the impossible for you.

Balak's troubled heart caused him to make a decision that proved to be destructive to his country. Jesus said, *Let not your heart be troubled* (John 14:1, KJV). God does not keep us from having troubles, but He commands us to not let our hearts be troubled.

How is it possible to keep a heart from being troubled? Our thoughts always precede our attitude. Before we make a decision, we think. Before we act, we think. Balak's thoughts caused him to be fearful of the Israelites. In chapters 2 and 3 of Deuteronomy, Moses had assured the leaders of the countries they needed to pass through that they would stay on the main roads and pay them in silver for any food they needed or any water they would drink. Instead of cooperating with Moses or seeking counsel from God, Balak made decisions based on his fear, or his troubled heart. If we are afraid, loving, anxious, peaceful, troubled, or filled by any other such feeling, it is the result of our thinking. Our attitude at all times is determined by our thoughts.

How can we obey the command *Let not your heart be troubled?* In his book *Hearing God,* Peter Lord gives us this word picture: Is it possible to get all the air out of a glass? Yes, it is easy. Just fill the glass with water. Is it possible to control our thoughts? Can we *take captive every thought* (2 Corinthians 10:5)? Yes, that can be easy, too, if we fill our minds with different thoughts. The principle is the same as filling a glass with water to get rid of the air.

There are three simple facts concerning thinking:
1. We cannot choose not to think.
2. We cannot think two thoughts at the same time.
3. We can choose our thoughts.

All thoughts can be divided into two basic categories: true or false. We have seen in Nehemiah's life his choice to believe God's plan and to refuse to think about the accusations and criticisms from his enemies. Thoughts that come from God are true. He is the source of all truth. From His holy Scriptures come truths that must become the focus of our daily lives and the pattern for our thought life. He has sent the Holy Spirit to dwell in us and to guide us into all truth.

How do you get the air out of the glass? By filling it with water. How do you get rid of wrong and untrue thoughts? By filling our minds with God's truths and His principles for our lives. The apostle Paul gave us a powerful bit of instruction to help us begin a correction in our thinking: *Whatever is true, whatever is noble,*

whatever is right, whatever is pure, whatever is lovely, whatever is admirable—if anything is excellent or praiseworthy—think about such things (Philippians 4:8).

Is there an area of your life in which your heart is troubled? Take a moment to consider the words of Jesus in John 14:1: *Do not let your hearts be troubled. Trust in God; trust also in me.*

Pray and ask the Holy Spirit to help you to trust Him as you begin to make corrections and fill your mind with right thoughts.

Written by Marie Coody

MEMORY CHALLENGE

Write Psalm 1:5 from memory.

Nehemiah

LESSON 10

■ A study of Nehemiah 13:6-31

Result of Disobedience

Read Nehemiah 13:4-5.

In the last chapter of Nehemiah we learn that even the best intentions of the perfect community under ideal leadership can fail and the people can lapse into sin.

1. Who was Eliashib?

2. What was Eliashib's responsibility?

3. What had he done for Tobiah, the Ammonite?

4. What had been the attitude of Tobiah regarding the repairing of the wall of Jerusalem? Summarize the following scriptures for the answer:

    Nehemiah 2:10

    Nehemiah 4:3

    Nehemiah 4:7

5. According to the Law of the Israelites, what should have been Eliashib's action toward Tobiah? (Nehemiah 13:1-3).

Eliashib, the high priest, was with the priests who rebuilt the Sheep Gate in the walls of Jerusalem. He would have known of Tobiah's opposition to the repair of the wall (Nehemiah 3:1, 20-21). After his appointment as supervisor of contributions, following the command and example of David (12:44-47), Eliashib could assign chambers in the Temple to whoever he pleased. He decided to assign a chamber of the Temple to Tobiah, to whom he was related by marriage.

6. How had the Temple chamber been used before Tobiah occupied it?

7. Who was designated to receive supplies from the offerings and contributions being stored in the Temple storerooms?

Eliashib saw the need for his relative, Tobiah, to have a place to stay when he came to Jerusalem; he could make a place for Tobiah in the Temple storeroom. In his own human understanding, this was a good thing to do, but he was giving no regard to the laws of Moses, which called for a separation of Jews and Gentiles.

Psalm 1:6

For the LORD watches over the way of the righteous, but the way of the wicked will perish.

(NIV)

Sometimes God's laws don't make sense from our human perspective, but like a loving parent, He sets standards for our good and protection from evil and harm.

8. Summarize the following scriptures, which admonish us to obey:

Deuteronomy 26:16

1 Samuel 15:22

Matthew 7:21

Acts 5:29

9. These scriptures warn of the penalties for disobedience. Summarize them.

Deuteronomy 11:26-28

1 Samuel 12:15

Ephesians 5:6

Hebrews 2:1-3

God desires obedience motivated not by fear but by love and trust. Obedience actually frees us to enjoy life as God intended, because it keeps us from becoming entangled or enslaved to those things that distract us and cause us problems and heartaches.

We expect God to be faithful to keep His word. Why do we tend to think we have the privilege of not obeying Him but still deserve His blessing and answers to our prayers?

The Book of Jonah is a wonderful biblical illustration of disobedience. If you haven't read it recently, take time to scan the four short chapters of Jonah, and review the reluctant missionary's flight from God. God's call to Jonah was, *Go to the great city of Nineveh, and preach against it, because its wickedness has come up before me* (Jonah 1:2).

The Assyrians were ruthless and barbaric military conquerors at that time. Their religious practices were unspeakably vile, with their cult fertility marked by licentiousness and perversity. The filth of their worship and their inhuman child sacrifices had not gone unnoticed by God. He was fed up with their depraved degeneracy and heartless cruelty. Jonah's reluctance to go and preach a message of judgment and doom in Nineveh is understandable.

Jonah decided to run away from the presence of the Lord. He chose to go to Tarsus, in Spain, 2,000 miles west. The story continues with a series of "downs."
> He went down to the seaport of Joppa;
> down into a ship;
> down into the hold of the ship and slept;
> down into the sea;
> down into the belly of a great fish, who spat him out on dry land three days later.

From inside the fish Jonah began to pray.

10. Read and summarize Psalm 139:7-12.

The Book of Jonah closes without revealing the end of Jonah's life. Neither do we know the final result of God's dealing with Eliashib in his disobedience. But we do know we have a tenacious God, who pursues all people with undying love.

The Book of Jonah is not a fish story but a narrative of a man who tried to run from God to avoid obeying Him. It powerfully illustrates the fact that God will find us wherever we go, no matter how far away or how remote we are. For Jonah, it took a storm and a great fish to learn obedience. For us, God will send an entirely different situation designed to teach us to obey Him. It could be any one of a hundred unexpected circumstances.

Is there an area of your life today in which you, like Jonah, are running from God? Or like Eliashib, have you taken things into your own hands and disobeyed His Word? Most likely, you will not be swallowed by a great fish. There is no Nehemiah to dictate the laws to you. But the Holy Spirit is wanting to guide you and empower you to correct any error in your life. Quiet your heart and mind today to sense His direction as you study His precious Word.

Righteous Stand

Read Nehemiah 13:6-9.

1. Where was Nehemiah at this time?

2. When Nehemiah returned to Jerusalem, what did he learn about the Temple?

3. In Ezra 10:24, who was listed as having married a foreign woman?

4. What was Nehemiah's reaction to Tobiah living in the Temple?

5. Nehemiah was not afraid to take a stand for what was right. Summarize John 2:13-16.

6. What orders did Nehemiah give in 13:9?

7. Summarize 1 Chronicles 23:27-28.

8. What was returned to its proper place in the Temple storerooms?

In 432 B.C., after governing Judah for 12 years, Nehemiah had returned to King Artaxerxes in Babylon. He apparently stayed in Babylon for several years. When he returned to Jerusalem, he was appalled at the sinful state of affairs.

During Nehemiah's first time in Jerusalem, he displayed great strength and courage as he met opposition and dealt with it head on as he restored the city wall. In his second time in Jerusalem, the same determination and courage served him well as he sought to bring reforms to the Jewish community. He threw out a Gentile who was permitted to live in the Temple; he restored the practice of tithing to support the Levites; he corrected Sabbath wrongs by those who bought and sold on the Sabbath; and he dealt forthrightly with those who had married foreigners. He was bold to take a stand when God's laws were being abused.

What is required when believers take a stand to live godly lives before the world? Charles Sheldon took a stand for Jesus Christ when he wrote the book *In His Steps*. His book is based on 1 Peter 2:21, which tells us, *To this you were called, because Christ suffered for you, leaving you an example, that you should follow in his steps.*

In the book, Henry Maxwell, respected pastor of the First Church of Raymond, struggled with the idea that Christian discipleship demanded more than mental assent. His church was the leading church in the city. It had the best choir. Its membership was composed of community leaders, representatives of the wealth, society, and intelligence of Raymond. After being deeply moved by a transient painter's tragic and untimely death, Dr. Maxwell vowed to preface every attitude and action of his own life with the question "What would Jesus do in this situation if He were me?"

After careful consideration, he challenged members of First Church by declaring, "I want volunteers from First Church who will pledge themselves, earnestly and honestly for an entire year, not to do anything without first asking the question, 'What would Jesus do?' and after asking the question, each one will follow Jesus as exactly as he knows how, no matter what the result would be. Our motto will be 'What would Jesus do?' Our aim will be to act as He would if He was in our places, regardless of immediate results. In other words, we propose to follow in Jesus' steps as closely and as literally as we believe He taught His disciples to do."

Through Henry Maxwell, Charles Sheldon (1857—1946) took a stand for righteousness. *In His Steps* was first published in 1896. By 1967, 30,000,000 copies had been sold. By taking a stand to challenge others to obey Scripture, Sheldon has encouraged millions to live fuller and more Christlike lives. Going into the 21st century, Sheldon's work is still an influence for godly principles. Many children, teens, and adults today wear the popular bracelets inscribed with the letters WWJD, an abbreviation for "What Would Jesus Do?"

Scripture admonishes us to be aware of situations in our lives in which we can take a stand for righteousness and make a difference—even when it is painful or difficult. Ephesians 6:13 says, *Therefore put on the full armor of God, so that when the day of evil comes, you may be able to stand your ground, and after you have done everything, to stand.* Nehemiah stood his ground when he came against evil. After he had done everything, he stood tall!

MEMORY CHALLENGE

Look up into the heavens and know that the Lord watches over the way of the righteous.

Restored Tithing

Read Nehemiah 13:10-14.

1. According to verse 10, what problem had Nehemiah learned about the Levites, and what action had they taken to solve the problem?

2. In verse 11, Nehemiah responded to the people's neglect of fulfilling the commands of the Law. List two steps he took to begin to reestablish order in the Temple.

3. How did Judah tithe?

4. Read Malachi 3:7-10; then summarize verse 10.

5. Nehemiah put these men in charge of the store-rooms:

   _____, the priest
   _____, the scribe
   _____, the Levite
   _____, their assistant

6. Why did he choose these men, and what was their responsibility?

7. Record Nehemiah's prayer to God (verse 14).

8. In Matthew 23:23, Jesus rebuked the Pharisees for their meticulous tithing on the one hand while on the other neglecting *the more important matters of the law,* namely _____, _____, and _____.

While the Old Testament specifically talks about giving to God one-tenth of what we earn, the New Testament encourages us to give what we can, to give sacrificially, and to give out of a grateful heart. For many, this means giving far more than one-tenth. One of the great promises of the Bible is that the more we give, the more we receive—not necessarily in material possessions, but in spiritual and eternal rewards.

Tithing begins with surrendering to the Lord. Giving of ourselves comes before giving of our substance. When we belong to the Lord wholeheartedly, we begin looking for opportunities to give instead of excuses not to give.

Tithing is a testimony to others of our commitment to the Lord and His principles for living. There are those who ridicule Christians who tithe, but God's blessings and the peace that obedience brings far outweigh the effects of any persecution from the world. When we rob God, we only rob ourselves. We cannot keep anything that rightfully belongs to God.

Tithing should be done gladly. *God loves a cheerful giver* (2 Corinthians 9:7). To receive spiritual enrichment from our tithing, we must be joyful and glad for other opportunities to give.

When we consider God's promises to faithful givers, how can we lose?

Ecclesiastes 11:1 (TLB)—*Give generously, for your gifts will return to you later.*

Matthew 10:42—*And if anyone gives even a cup of cold water to one of these little ones because he is my disciple, I tell you the truth, he will certainly not lose his reward.*

Luke 6:38—*Give, and it will be given to you. A good measure, pressed down, shaken together and running over, will be poured into your lap. For with the measure you use, it will be measured to you.*

Acts 20:35—*Jesus himself said, "It is more blessed to give than to receive."*

Chrysostom, one of the Early Church fathers, wrote, "Someone told me with great amazement that so-and-so gives a tithe. How shameful it is that what was taken for granted among the Jews has become an amazing thing among Christians. And if non-payment of the tithe puts a man in jeopardy with God, then consider how many are in danger today."

God hasn't changed His laws. Radical obedience includes tithing. Tithing demonstrates that God is first in our lives.

MEMORY CHALLENGE

Prayerfully sorrow over the wicked who will perish.

Reform of the Sabbath

Read Nehemiah 13:15-22.

1. What was happening in Jerusalem on the Sabbath?

2. Read Nehemiah 10:31 and record the agreement with Ezra regarding the Sabbath.

3. Summarize these Scriptures regarding God's instructions on the Sabbath:

   Exodus 34:21

   Deuteronomy 5:12-15

   Jeremiah 17:21-23, 27

4. What did Nehemiah say to rebuke the nobles of Judah?

5. Review Nehemiah 13:19 and summarize how Nehemiah began to correct the desecration of the Sabbath, including his warning to the merchants.

6. In order to keep the Sabbath holy, Nehemiah had stationed his own men at the gates (verse 19) so that merchandise could not be brought in to sell on the Sabbath. Later he replaced his own men with others. Who were they?

7. Read Exodus 20:8-11. How many people are to work on the Sabbath?

8. Using Nehemiah's prayer in verse 22 as a model, personalize this prayer for yourself.

There can be no doubt concerning the fourth commandment, which tells us to *Remember the Sabbath day by keeping it holy* (Exodus 20:8). It is referred to many times in the Scriptures. Does this commandment require the same radical obedience for us that it did for Nehemiah and Israel?

How would Jesus observe the Sabbath in the 21st century? What do you do on your Sabbath? What does it mean to keep a day holy?

One of the definitions of "holy" is "set apart from the ordinary." Our Sabbath is to be set apart from the ordinary six days of a week. God modeled this for us at Creation. He rested on the seventh day. We are to have a 24-hour Sabbath after six days of labor. We are made to need a day of rest after a week of work. We are more productive the other six days if we have a day of rest during the week. On the Sabbath we are to rest. Our bodies need to be renewed; our energy needs to be restored.

A day set apart from the working week can also bring health to our emotions. We need relief from pressures of the weekdays. We need time for quietness. Jesus and His disciples took time to be away from the crowds. We need to be led by *the still waters* (Psalm 23:2, KJV) and to *be still, and know that I am God* (Psalm 46:10). We can relax with family and friends and encourage one another. We should include time to cultivate opportunities to be together with other believers. As we bear one another's burdens, the pressures are lessened. As we share our joys, we are strengthened. Nehemiah said, *The joy of the LORD is your strength* (Nehemiah 8:10).

Twenty-two percent of the people who live in the United States work on the Sabbath—medical professionals, pastors, transportation employees, and so on. These people should observe the fourth commandment on another day of the week.

As we set apart and value the Sabbath, we will make it a day for remembering who God is and where we stand in our personal walk with Him. Psalm 95:1-2, 6-7 gives us a pattern for Sabbath day worship:
> *Come, let us sing for joy to the LORD;*
> *let us shout aloud to the Rock of our salvation.*

*Let us come before him with thanksgiving
and extol him with music and song. . . .*

*Come, let us bow down in worship,
let us kneel before the LORD our Maker;
for he is our God
and we are the people of his pasture,
the flock under his care.*

Each one of us is a part of *the flock under His care.* He knows we are battered by our ungodly culture and that we need to focus in on Him, His values, and His principles. In Matthew 11:28 He tells us to come to Him when we are weary and burdened and He will give us rest.

As we gather together on the Sabbath for a study of His Word and to worship together, He will meet with us and bless us. He will empower us for the days ahead. We must not lose our spiritual momentum by neglecting the Lord on the Sabbath. We must establish this spiritual discipline of observing the Sabbath day and keeping it holy.

In making God first, give Him the first day of the week. The high point of every week for the believer should be the Lord's Day.

Dear Heavenly Father, help us to cherish Your Sabbath as You do.

(Portions of this day's lesson are condensed from a sermon by Melvin McCullough titled "God's Word to Workaholics.")

MEMORY CHALLENGE

Write the verse several times until you are beginning to memorize it.

DAY FIVE
Rebuked Mixed Marriages

Read Nehemiah 13:23-30.

1. What were the men of Judah doing that was wrong?

2. How had the mixed marriages influenced the languages of the children?

3. Read Malachi 2:10-11. Record the words pertaining to marriage.

4. What command did the Lord give (in Deuteronomy 7:1-4) regarding marrying foreign women?

Thirty years have elapsed since Ezra's reforms in 458 B.C. This tells us that there has been enough time for a completely new generation to grow up, mixed marriages to be contracted, and children of those marriages to have learned to talk. Nehemiah was concerned because so many of the children were unable to speak the Hebrew language. However, that was not the real reason for his anger. He was appalled because he knew that mixed marriages would endanger the existence of the Jewish community (verse 18) and were acts of disloyalty to God. Nehemiah 13:28 tells us that the son of Joiada was expelled. This was necessary because the priestly line was not to be contaminated by intermarriage.

Foreign wives presented a grave threat to the spiritual integrity of the covenantal faith because of their general unwillingness to turn from their national deities when they married Jews. To a large extent, it was the women who perpetuated the religious traditions of the time and trained their children to follow their ways. This situation continues to exist today in some Asian countries, where the women are still regarded as responsible for maintaining the integrity of the religious and social traditions of the particular culture involved.

5. In chapter 10 of Ezra, men were ordered to leave their foreign wives. Years later, the same marital involvements occurred again. How did Nehemiah confront the men in Nehemiah 13:25?

The religious reforms that Ezra instituted regarding mixed marriages caused a considerable amount of social and personal upheaval. Necessary as it was for their spiritual stability, it could only be carried to completion by the authoritative backing of Nehemiah, who evidently remained in office until 433 B.C.

6. Who are the men of Judah being compared to?

Solomon was the son of David and Bathsheba (2 Samuel 12). His father, David, was a brilliant man who, for the greatest part of his life, was a devoted man of God. Considering the times in which he lived, Solomon began his reign as king well but made a foolish choice in choosing a foreign king's daughter for his wife (1 Kings 3:1). It may have been a wise political move but proved to have much to do later with his moral downfall.

Early in Solomon's reign, the Lord spoke to him and told him to ask for anything that he wanted. Solomon asked for an understanding heart, and the Lord granted his request. Solomon became not only the wisest man of all time but also the wealthiest and most honored king of his day.

As he increased in wealth and honor, he desired to have the world see his riches. He lived a most luxurious and extravagant lifestyle beyond what his country could afford, and this caused unrest in the kingdom. In later years, his life of sensuality and the influence of many wives caused him to introduce worship of false gods into Jerusalem.

Nehemiah's use of Solomon as an example to the men of Judah should have been a great warning to them. Solomon was known as the wisest man, yet his wisdom did not teach him self-control. He taught well but failed to practice what he taught. Solomon describes the fool in many verses of the Book of Proverbs and shows us a picture of his own weaknesses and failures.

Solomon was a guidepost rather than an example. He wanted the way to wisdom, but in the latter part of his life he did not walk in it; hence his son, Rehoboam, followed his example, rather than his counsel, and became a foolish and evil ruler.

To be a godly example before our families and others is a constant challenge. We have been reminded this week to consider, "What would Jesus do?" in every decision of our lives. Are we searching our hearts? Let no sin come between us and our God.

MEMORY CHALLENGE

Begin to add this verse to those you have memorized earlier.

Remember Nehemiah

Scriptures to be read for today's lesson will be designated with the questions that follow.

On this last day of our study of Nehemiah, we will select some of the qualities of this patriotic statesman to help us apply them to our lives today. Our responsibilities are very different from that of building a city wall, but we can face similar confrontations from evil. Nehemiah's extraordinary ability to solve problems was a direct result of the fact that he was a man of prayer. He is a valuable model to us because as he turned to God, he received answers to seemingly impossible obstacles. He had a heart that habitually sought strength and wisdom from his Heavenly Father.

Consider the following obstacles that, with God's help, Nehemiah was able to overcome. Think about how his problem-solving techniques might be useful to us today as we work toward our own spiritual maturity.

1. **Ridicule**
   Read Nehemiah 2:19-20.
   How did Nehemiah overcome ridicule for his plan to rebuild the wall?

2. **Anger**
   Read Nehemiah 4:3-6.
   Record two ways Nehemiah and the workers overcame anger.

3. **Conspiracy**
   Read Nehemiah 4:7-9.
   Record two ways the threat was met.

4. **Discouragement of friends and enemies**
   Read Nehemiah 4:10-14.
   Record two actions that solved the problem.

5. **Greed**
   Read Nehemiah 5:1-17.
   Record how the selfish greed of the leaders was overcome (verse 12).

6. Schemes against us
Read Nehemiah 6:1-16.
List some ways that show how the schemes against them were defeated.

In the restoration of the Jews from their captivity in Babylon, God used three capable leaders:

a prince, Zerubbabel, with the first group to return	538 B.C.
a priest, Ezra, with the second return	458 B.C.
a layman, Nehemiah, with the third return	444 B.C.

Nehemiah was not a priest like Ezra or a member of the nobility like Zerubbabel. He was a layman who probably had been a successful businessman in Babylon while in captivity. After becoming wealthy, he entered governmental service in the land of his captivity. His position as cupbearer to King Artaxerxes brought Nehemiah into close daily contact with the king himself. Because of his relationship with the king, Nehemiah was released and given supplies to return to Jerusalem.

Nehemiah made two visits from King Artaxerxes to Jerusalem (2:1-6; 13:6-7). His first, in 445 B.C., was to repair the walls; they were in a state of disrepair almost a century after the first arrival from exile in 538 B.C. The second was a problem-solving trip in the 32nd year of Artaxerxes, reign (13:6), 432 B.C. Nehemiah was a contemporary of Ezra and Malachi, and also Socrates in Greece (470-399 B.C.), and only a few decades later than Gautama Buddha in India (560-480 B.C.) and Confucius in China (551-479 B.C.).

In the 12 years of Nehemiah's stay in Jerusalem, he showed outstanding leadership abilities and was totally committed to God. As a leader he demonstrated excellent engineering knowledge and brilliant organizational and motivational abilities (chapter 3).

Building the walls caused a labor shortage; farms were mortgaged, and high rates of interest were charged. Nehemiah said, *What you are doing is not right* (5:9). He corrected the problem and even gave financial aid to those in need. Several attempts were made to lure Nehemiah away from the job and shut it down, but they failed. Nehemiah proved to be a person of strong will and unusual boldness. *So the wall was completed . . . in fifty-two days* (6:15).

Nehemiah was indeed an outstanding person. His theology was very practical; it affected every area of his life. We have read his prayers and have seen how practical they were. During the Great Revival (Nehemiah 8—10), people made confession and worshiped the Lord (9:3). The signers and terms of the covenant were then recorded (chapter 10).

Nehemiah was dissatisfied with the small size of Jerusalem. He made an ingenious proposal: to *cast lots to bring one out of every ten to live in Jerusalem, the holy city, while the remaining nine were to stay in their own towns* (11:1).

Nehemiah's last chapter records his reforms during his second visit to Jerusalem in 432 B.C. He believed *the God of heaven will give us success* (2:20) and that *our God will fight for us!* (4:20). He had respect for the Sabbath, the Temple and its institutions, the Levites and tithing.

God gave Nehemiah a task that required great perseverance. He was able to persevere because of his love for the people of God. He unwaveringly persevered by pursuing his goal in spite of the contempt generated by the work and continued in spite of the hatred and opposition of enemies and the fainthearted ness of fellow-laborers (4:8-11). He gave himself up entirely to the work, baffled all the schemes of the enemy, and avoided every snare because God took care of those who trusted in Him. Encouraged by Nehemiah's determination and energy, the people were ready to work and fight at the same time in order to get the work done.

Nehemiah was an unusual person. He was a man of action who knew how to use persuasion as well as force. We may properly call him the father of Judaism. Because of Nehemiah, Judaism had a fortified city, a purified people, a dedicated and unified nation, renewed economic stability, and a new commitment to God's Law.

Nehemiah is a part of a faithful remnant who fear the Lord, obey Him, ponder His truth, and exercise spiritual discernment. God uses those people and keeps a record of their names. They are His jewels, and they will be spared in the coming day of judgment.

Dear Lord, looking at the life of Nehemiah challenges me to persevere in Your call on my life. Remember me, O God, along with Your servant Nehemiah.

Written by Marie Coody

MEMORY CHALLENGE

Repeat Psalm 1 aloud until you understand and know it.